Cooking Aboard a Small Boat

Feeding the Small Boat Sailor

Cooking Aboard a Small Boat

Feeding the Small Boat Sailor

No man will be a sailor who has contrivance enough
to get himself into a jail; for being in ship is being in
a jail, with the chance of being drowned ... A man in
a jail has more room, better food, and commonly
better company.
(Samuel Johnson [1709-1784], *Boswell Life* 1759)

Paul Esterle

Published 2012

Printed by Capt'n Pauley Productions in the United States of America

ISBN 978-1-105-73632-2

Capt'n Pauley Productions
4142 Ogletown-Stanton Rd.
#243
Newark DE 19713

Acknowledgements

The idea for this book springs from a chance comment from Josh Colvin and Craig Wagner, editors and publishers of Small Craft Advisor magazine. While kicking around several ideas for future columns (I'm technical editor there) they mentioned that there might some interest is revisiting some of my old columns about cooking aboard Ternabout, our small fiberglass sailboat.

The more I thought about it, the more I became convinced that an article or two wouldn't do the subject justice. Cooking aboard a small boat is totally different from doing so aboard a larger boat with a dedicated galley, no matter how small that galley might be. The extensive time I spent aboard Ternabout convinced me that you can eat well aboard even the smallest craft if you are organized and prepared. This book is the end result of those comments, thoughts and experiences.

I would also be remiss if I didn't thank my trusty crew for their years of being my guinea pigs: daughter Becky, son Eric and my wife. Pat. Becky has gone on to be a dedicated sailor and racer with more sea time that Dad. Eric's idea of cruising tends towards larger craft with Disney emblazoned on the side. In addition to serving as my taster, Pat has been my indefatigable proof reader for this book as well as my other articles and boats. I thank you all.

Preface

In most of the past sections, I've talked about upgrades that involved modifying or adding to the boat's structure. Let's change tacks for a while and talk about something near and dear to all of our hearts – FOOD! To be more precise, I'll cover some tools, equipment and tips and then deal with food, cooking and some recipes. (Yes, Virginia, the Capt'n CAN cook!)

Cooking aboard a small craft may not be as convenient as opening up the fridge and firing up the stove at home, but it also doesn't mean starvation rations, either. Careful planning, efficient use of space and practice can make the food aboard as enjoyable as what you prepare at home. In fact, more so, after all, you ARE out on the water!

Paul Esterle

Table of Contents

Chapter 1: Introduction

Food has always been an integral part of my family's sailing life. Part of that was due to my son. We would go down to the boat on a weekend. He would walk down the dock and prepare to board the boat. He would raise one foot preparing to board, but before that foot had a chance to land on the boat, he'd ask, "What's there to eat?" A true mobile appetite.

After I put Ternabout, our 20-foot sloop, in a marina slip in Tennessee, I began spending more time aboard, weekends and as much other time as I could get. There was no marina restaurant or even a close place to grab a quick meal, so eating aboard became a necessity. Given the fact that Ternabout has a very minimal galley and no refrigeration, I began experimenting with various means of cooking aboard without those luxuries.

My fellow boaters, subsisting on chips and stale sandwiches, were always amazed at what I could prepare and serve, given the limited facilities aboard. Part of that is due to the unavoidable fact that food always tastes best when served by someone else and out on the water.

In any case, all those years of experience are distilled here in this book. As always, it isn't the only way of doing things or even necessarily the best, but it's what has worked for me over the years. Enjoy!

Old Time Sailor Fare

Back in the age of sail, it was "wooden ships and iron men." Not the least part of those iron men were their iron stomachs. They had to be to be able survive on the food they carried aboard; salt pork and beef, weevil-riddled hard tack, little fresh food and stagnant water. No wonder the Royal Navy served a daily ration of grog (rum and water).

I remember the scene from the movie "Master and Commander" where the ship's officers were sitting around the mess table discussing the weevils in the ships biscuit. "Always choose the lesser of two weevils", was the advice from Captain Jack Aubrey. As it turns out, the "weevily biscuit" is largely an exaggeration for dramatic effect.

Figure 1: Hard tack or ship's biscuit; not a weevil in sight..

Still, the diet was monotonous with only brief treats like dried apple pies and plum duff. Hard tack or ships biscuits, soaked in water, then fried up in rancid grease with salt cod or salt pork was common. Lobscouse was a coarse stew of salt beef, dried vegetables and hard tack.

Sounds appetizing, right? The lack of fresh fruits and vegetables resulted in nutritionally related diseases like scurvy. It's no accident that British sailors were called "limeys", after it was discovered that regular doses of lime juice would keep scurvy at bay.

Sailing was strictly a means of trade and livelihood up until the mid-1800s, when people began sailing, and racing, recreationally. The food situation improved somewhat in that most recreational sailing was done near the coast and access to fresh food supplies ashore was much better, Cooking aboard didn't change a whole lot though. One view of cooking aboard these craft can be gained by reading L. Francis Herreshoff's classic, Sensible Cruising Designs.

Dinty Moore

Recreational sailing became much more popular after World War II and the rise of an affluent middle class, coupled with relatively inexpensive fiberglass boats. I call that the era of Dinty Moore. Dinty Moore is a canned beef stew that was popular at that time. Compact, cheap and portable, all you had to do was open a can and heat it up for a hot meal aboard. I guess that it wasn't too bad for GI's used to canned "C" rations.

Figure 2: Almost every boat has a can aboard

Dinty Moore is still available today, in a wide variety of flavors, and is still carried aboard many boats – as emergency fare. If you get creative with your spices and a little wine, it really isn't bad, considering the convenience factor. It is hardly gourmet fare, though.

Sandwiches, Sandwiches, Sandwiches and Chips

Once lightweight, well insulated plastic coolers became available, the fare turned to sandwiches (does anyone besides me remember that the first Coleman coolers were metal and heavy as all get out?).

Figure 3: An early, metal, Coleman cooler - HEAVY!

Made ahead of time and placed in ice-filled coolers, they became the staples of the recreational sailor. Coupled with a bag of chips, most sailors were at least not hungry. While they were at least fresh and mostly wholesome, they did get boring after a while. They had the advantage of being quick and easy to make, from supplies usually on hand at home.

Better Food, Happier Sailors

That brings us to the reason for this book. The sandwiches and Dinty Moore work for a while, but sooner or later we get a hankering for better grub. The whole reason for this book is to show you how to provide that better fare from even the smallest and minimal galley.

Cooking Aboard a Small Boat

There are a lot of galley books and boating cookbooks out there. However, there aren't many, if any dealing with cooking aboard a small boat. Most of our boats don't have refrigeration units, permanent stove installations, water systems or electrical systems aboard. Many would-be cooks find that a little intimidating. This book is here to show you how to live well aboard, for extended periods if you like, while enjoying good food afloat.

Chapter 2: Cooking Fuels and Stoves

While sandwiches and cold cuts will suffice for a while, sooner or later you'll want some heat, for your morning coffee, a tasty entrée or a warming soup on a cold afternoon. That will require some sort of stove, of which you have several choices. Let's look at some of the more popular ones and their pros and cons.

Stoves commonly used aboard boats can be divided into six categories based on the energy source:

Propane
Butane
Alcohol
Kerosene
Solid Fuel
Combination Stoves

Each of these fuel types have different BTU content. A BTU (British Thermal Unit) is defined as the amount of heat required to raise the temperature of one pound of water by one degree (F). While hard to visualize, it is a handy means of comparing fuels and stove outputs. The following table shows the approximate BTU content, per gallon, of common stove fuels:

Propane   91,000 BTU/Gal.
Butane   102,000 BTU/Gal.
Kerosene   129,000 BTU/Gal.
Alcohol   65,000 BTU/Gal.

Cooking Aboard a Small Boat

Solid fuels are weighed by pound or volume and electricity is measured in kilowatt hours, making it difficult to compare with liquid fuels

While important, the fuel type isn't the only criteria for choosing a stove for your boat. Fuel cost and availability, fuel safety factors, stove cost and ease of use all figure into your choice. Other factors are also important: many people don't like the smell of kerosene, might be afraid of propane or don't want to deal with the ash from a solid fuel stove. Often the choice is made for you when the stove comes with the boat. As long as the stove is safe, give it a try and see how you like it before deciding to switch styles.

Propane

Propane is probably one of the most popular cooking fuels used aboard boats. It is relatively cheap, easy to find and produces a lot of heat. There are also a wide variety of propane stoves available, from permanent marine installations to modest backpacker models and everything in between. Propane does have its problems. It is a gas that is heavier than air and will sink to the lowest sections of the bilge. If sufficient vapors accumulate and reach an ignition source, an explosion will result. For that reason permanent marine propane installations are tightly governed by ABYC (American Boat and Yacht Council) and National Fire Protection Association regulations.

Propane stoves can be grouped into two categories, permanent installations and portable units.

Permanently Installed Propane Stoves

As mentioned above, the installation of these stoves is strictly regulated. A dedicated propane locker is required, with an overboard drain for any propane fumes. A regulator is required to reduce the high pressure propane from the tank down to the low pressure required by the stove. An electric gas shut off solenoid is also required. Both of these items must be installed inside the propane locker. A continuous propane line must run from inside the propane locker to the stove with no connections in between. The line must be protected from chafe where it passes through a bulkhead and the line should be

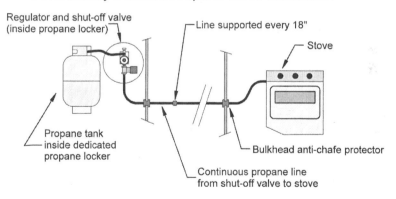

Permenantly Installed Propane Stove Installation

supported at least every 18″. There needs to be a switch to remotely activate the shut off solenoid located next to the stove. Propane "sniffers" should be installed to warn of any accumulation of propane gas in the bilge and sound an alarm if necessary.

The common gimbaled propane marine stove will be a little over 20" wide, 20"+ high and almost as deep, a hefty space requirement. For that amount of space, you'll get two or three burners, an oven and often a broiler to boot. It is also a significant investment, running anywhere from $900 and up, some to over $4,000. This is for the stove only, not counting installation labor and materials. For most of us, such an installation is out of the question unless it came with the boat.

Portable Propane Stoves

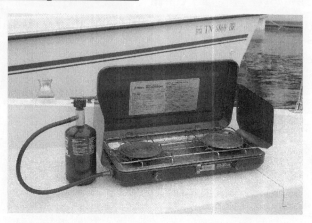

Figure 4: Ternabout;'s trusty (and slightly rusty(Coleman propane stove.

Chapter 2: Cooking Fuels and Stoves

A portable propane stove is a much more viable option for most of our boats. The popularity of camping and RVing has produced a number of good, inexpensive stoves using the small, portable propane cylinders. In fact, many of us have switched from the "white gas" fueled Coleman two-burner stoves we used when camping to its propane powered brothers.

For safety's sake, these stoves should be used in an open cockpit. Using one below decks runs the risks of propane leaks and carbon monoxide buildup. Likewise, propane cylinders should only be stored outside in a propane bag or storage device (see next section on how to build your own).

The most common two-burner style propane stove is light, compact and has a stable, low center of gravity. You can find these in the camping section of most discount stores, from around $50 and up. At these prices, they aren't made from marine grade materials, most are stamped sheet metal. I can tell you that my Coleman has been going on for over thirty years with no problems.

There are also many designs of single burner back-packing and camping stoves. These are great for one pot meals on a stable, flat surface. Most are too tall for stable use aboard a moving, rocking boat. The one exception is the Forespar "Hot Spot Mini Galley". This single burner stove uses a small propane cylinder and has a three-way gimbal mounting. It is designed to be attached to a vertical bulkhead and will gimbal with the motion of the boat. With a stainless steel coffee/cook pot and a removable mounting bracket, this stove will set you back about $130.

Figure 5: The Forespar Mini Hot Spot stove (photo courtesy of Forespar).

As I mentioned, I have used my two-burner Coleman stove aboard Ternabout for years. It heats quickly and cooks well, at times, too well. I found that the propane burners concentrate heat on a relatively small area of the pot or pan, resulting in uneven heating across the width of the pan. Luckily, others must have had the same problem as there is a ready solution. I purchased "flame tamers: from a camping stove and permanently wired them to the stove grate above the burner. These tamers are sheet metal disks that even out the heat from the burner and provide uniform heat to the bottom of my cooking pot or pan. Well worth the couple of bucks they cost. I used Monel safety wire to permanently fix them to the grate.

Figure 6: The flame tamer wired to my stove grate.

Most of these Coleman style stoves use side wings and the top cover as wind deflectors. This feature is very useful in a stove used in the open, sometimes breezy, cockpit. Make sure the stove you choose has this feature.

Gas Grills

Figure 7: A Magma propane grill, designed to mount on a stern pulpit (photo courtesy of Magma Products).

There is also a wide variety of propane grills designed for use aboard a boat. Most of these are designed to mount on a stern rail or pulpit and will hang over the side. This is a safety feature to allow you to dump any flaming contents into the water, not into the cockpit.

There are also mounts that are designed to fit in rod holders, should your boat come equipped with them. These units are great for grilling a steak but work less well for heating your coffee pot. In addition, they take

14

up valuable real estate on the stern rail, area that could be used for a boarding ladder or life ring.

There are also several different models of portable gas grills. These use the standard 14 oz. disposable propane cylinders. Prices range from around $24 to about $50, depending on the model. I loaded one aboard Ternabout when I was planning on a beach picnic. We'd beach the boat on a sandy beach and set the grill up onshore. Grilled sausages or hamburgers always tasted better outdoors. These units are usually lightweight stamped steel construction and cool off quickly after shutting down. None are marine grade but, at their low cost, you can afford to replace them every year, if need be. Not good to use to cook aboard but can't be beat for those shore-side picnics.

Fuel Safety

As I discussed above, my preferred cook stove aboard Ternabout is an "experienced" Hillary propane stove by Coleman. We have used it in our camping van, at picnics and aboard all our boats. The downside is that is does use propane as fuel. Propane is heavier than air and can collect in your bilge if kept below should a canister leak.

As a result, I store all my propane bottles outside in the cockpit, in a holder attached to the stern rail. There are two different styles, a flexible Sunbrella fabric one and one made from PVC. The fabric unit is made by Magma (the grill people) and lists for about $25. It is suspended from a horizontal rail on the stern rail.

The PVC unit I have on Ternabout was made by Stuart Swan Marine Corp. and was called a Propane Holster. It is designed to mount on a vertical stern rail support. I can't find a current listing for them so I don't know if they are still in business. It is a good candidate for home building in any case.

Both units allow leaking propane to safely vent over the side, preventing propane buildup in the bilge. Don't leave the dock without proper propane storage!

Building a Propane Storage Device

One trip to a local home improvement store should net most of the materials needed to build the device. A length of four-inch PVC pipe, two end caps, some stainless steel chain or a spare length of line and some PVC cement will be enough to get started.

Cut a piece of the PVC pipe to length. It should be long enough to hold two canisters, with the end caps in place. Glue the bottom end cap onto the pipe with the PVC cement. Drill a large hole in the bottom end cap to allow leaking propane to vent out of the holder. The top end cap is not glued (how would you get the cylinders out?).

A chain or length of light line is attached to the loose top cap with stainless steel nut and bolt or a knot on the inside of the cap. The other end will need to be permanently fastened, either to the holder or to the rail mounting.

There are a couple of ways of mounting the holder to the vertical stern rail. I used a couple of stamped stainless steel brackets normally used for lifeline terminations. They snapped around the tubing and had a hole I used to bolt the holder to the rail. I put the heads of the bolts inside the pipe so there was no interference with the propane cylinders.

Another option would be a pair of Helm Rail Mount Clamps. These things are extremely useful aboard a boat and I use them extensively aboard Ternabout. One end would need to be curved to match the pipe and slightly longer screws used, but they would work well.

A third mounting option would be to bend two brackets from 1/16″ x 1″ aluminum bar stock. These would then be bolted near the top and bottom of the pipe. Make them slightly smaller than the diameter of the stern rail so the holder is clamped in place.

Propane Cylinder Holder

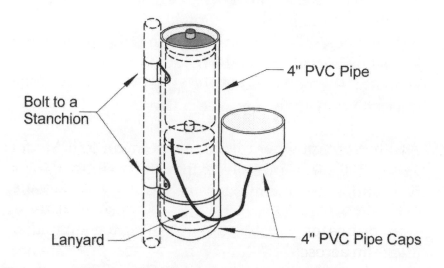

Bolt to a Stanchion

4" PVC Pipe

Lanyard

4" PVC Pipe Caps

Holds two 1-pound cylinders

My stamped stainless steel brackets and the home-made aluminum one will both require standoffs in the form or washers or something similar to space the pipe away from the vertical stern rail. There must be enough clearance so the top cap can easily be removed and replaced when accessing a cylinder.

The propane cylinders come with a protective plastic cap on the screw top connection. Make sure your cylinders have this in place. Dropping the top cylinder on top of unprotected threads on the cylinder beneath can result in a leaking cylinder or one that won't thread into the propane fitting.

If you use butane canisters for a butane stove, the same principles apply, just with different size PVC pipe.

Recap
If you are going to use propane aboard, (it is an excellent stove fuel) make sure you protect yourself and your boat by storing the propane cylinders properly.

Butane
There aren't a huge number of choices in the butane stove category. However, several of the ones that are available work very well aboard a small boat for a crew of one or two. All are single burner units that utilize an aerosol sized canister of butane. They are not made from marine friendly materials being largely sheet steel.

Figure 8: A typical butane stove and butane canister.

19

However, at the going price, under $20, you can replace the stove every year for years and still not cost as much as a marine-rated stove. Another advantage of butane is that it's high BTU content, providing a large amount of heat for the small size of the stove. There'll be no problem frying the bacon and eggs on this stove.

The butane canister slides into the stove. A safety interlock prevents you from inserting the canister unless the valve is in the off position. As with propane, the canisters should not be stored inside the cabin. Build yourself a storage container, similar to the one shown for propane cylinders and store in the open cockpit. A four pack of butane canisters costs around $9. A single canister should burn for over an hour or two on the high setting.

Like all stoves, combustion produces carbon monoxide so they should be used in well ventilated, preferably outside, locations. There are also many backpacking stoves designed to operate on butane. Most of these stoves utilize a non-standard gas canister. They are optimized for light weight and for use on flat, level and non-moving surfaces. Their tall design makes them dangerously unstable for use aboard a boat.

Not at all fancy but one of the inexpensive models makes a very useful stove for a smaller, space constrained boat.

Chapter 2: Cooking Fuels and Stoves

Alcohol

Alcohol is used by many, who consider it a safer fuel than butane or propane, for example. Alcohol has its own safety problems as alcohol flames in open air are hard to see, so spilled fuel can be very dangerous. Alcohol as a fuel has a lower BTU content than many other fuels and can be more expensive and/or hard to find. For example, the current price on stove alcohol at a marine store is in the neighborhood of $30/gallon verses about $4/gallon for propane.

There are two basic types of alcohol stoves: pressurized and unpressurized.

Pressurized Alcohol Stoves

These stoves deliver the alcohol to the stove burners under pressure. Most of them have the fuel delivery piping arranged so that it passes over the flame and the alcohol is vaporized before burning.

The stove system includes an alcohol tank installed remotely from the stove. There is a provision for pressurizing the tank; either by means of a simple bicycle pump or by a built-in pump. Once the alcohol tank is filled (there needs to be enough air space to build up pressure) and pressurized, you can light the stove.

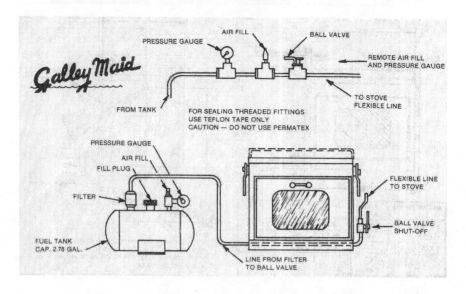

Some models suggest placing a small amount of fuel in a burner pan and lighting it. You then carefully turn on the burner. If you are successful, the alcohol will vaporize and the stove will light. If it fails to light, turn off the burner immediately as the unburnt alcohol is now forming a puddle in your stove. Trying to relight the stove at this point can result in an alcohol fire. One of my boats had such a pressurized system and the previous owner's wife had set the boat afire at least once, luckily not seriously.

Almost all pressurized stoves that I am familiar with are larger two or three burner units, often gimbaled and having an oven and/or broiler. These are too big to be installed aboard most of our boats.

Unpressurized Alcohol Stoves

For these reasons, almost all of the alcohol stoves used aboard smaller boats are unpressurized. Canisters under the burners contain a fire proof absorbent material that soaks up the alcohol as you fill the canister. This reduces any free alcohol to keep it from sloshing around and spilling. The burner atop the canister is simply lit and the alcohol begins to burn. Closing the lid on the burner shuts off the flame. Obviously flame control is less accurate than a pressurized system but, in my experience, we run them flat out anyway.

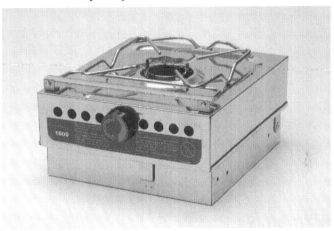

Figure 9: A single-burner, non-pressurized alcohol stove.

This process is much safer than a pressurized alcohol system, but, unfortunately, doesn't burn quite as hot. It is more than sufficient to prepare simple, quick meals, including that critical morning coffee (or tea).

Origo is a popular maker of unpressurized alcohol stoves. These are not cheap! A single burner Origo marine alcohol stove will set you back about $230. A two burner models runs right around $340. Many boats, especially power boats, have alcohol/electric stoves installed. Electric elements while at the dock and alcohol when you are away from shore power. Again, not cheap! A single burner runs about $340 while a two burner goes for a whopping $600+.

A final form of unpressurized alcohol stove is jellied alcohol canisters, commonly known as Sterno. These work okay for chafing dishes on land but are woefully lacking in BTU output for use aboard any size boat.

There are also several styles of alcohol stoves designed specifically for backpacking. These are usually pretty pricey and are designed to operate on a level, flat, non-moving surface. I would not trust them on a rocking boat, even at anchor.

While alcohol has a lower heat content than, say, gasoline, alcohol fires are still dangerous. Alcohol flams are nearly invisible burring in open air. Dousing an alcohol fire with water merely spreads it around,

Chapter 2: Cooking Fuels and Stoves

The following excerpt is from the MSDS (Material Safety Data Sheet) for denatured alcohol:

Extinguishing Media Use water spray, CO_2. Alcohol-type or universal type foams or dry chemical

Special Firefighting Procedures: The use of self-contained breathing apparatus is recommended for firefighters. Use water spray to cool fire exposed containers and structures/ Avoid spreading burning liquid with water used for cooling purposes. Ethanol vapors are heavier than air and may travel a considerable distance to a source of ignition and flash back. Alcohols burn with a pale blue flame which may be extremely hard to see under normal lighting conditions. Personnel may only be able to feel the heat of the fire without seeing flames. Extreme caution must be exercised in fighting alcohol fires. Fight fires for maximum distance of use unmanned hose holders or monitor nozzles. Cool containers with flooding quantities of water until well after fire is out. Withdraw immediately in case of rising sound from venting safety devices or discoloration of tank. Always stay away from tanks engulfed in fire.

Solid Fuel Stoves

In the past, all boats, commercial and recreational, used solid fuel stoves. Solid fuels encompass wood, coal, charcoal, wood pellets, even corn and corn cobs. These days only a few traditionalists use solid fuel stoves for cooking aboard their boats. Solid fuel stoves have the advantage of keeping the cabin warm and dry in cold weather and the disadvantage of keeping the cabin hot in warm weather. Most importantly, permanently solid fuel stoves are not approved for use aboard gasoline powered boats

Figure 10: A traditional solid fuel stove (photo courtesy of Navigator Stove Works, Inc.)

Most of these stoves are made from cast iron. For use in the marine environment, they should be ceramic coated as cast iron will rust quickly unless kept polished. Installations must be done properly with concern for spacing from combustible surfaces, proper chimneys and a workable Charlie Noble. For those of you not up on your nautical nomenclature, Charlie Noble is the top of the stove pipe extending from the deck. The design of this device is crucial to a properly drawing stove and minimizing back drafts.

Solid fuel stoves have problems of their own, Ash disposal is probably one of the most annoying. There are also the possibilities of staining the sails, deck or cabin top to deal with. Solid fuels have a tendency to build up soot in the stove pipe which can lead the chimney fires. These fires can be extremely hot, reaching several thousand degrees, and extremely hard to put out.

Solid fuel stoves should be matched to the type of fuel you intend to use. Wood stoves are common and can be fed from driftwood gathered on the beach. Bring a sharp saw and have plenty of storage space available for the wood. Coal is another option. Be sure to select a stove designed for coal. The main difference is in the grating. You should be able to shake it to cause ashes and clinker to drop into the ash pan. If the grate is fixed, you'll need a poker to stir the ash into the ash pan. If you want to burn multiple fuel types make sure the stove is rated as a multi-fuel stove.

If you are installing the stove yourself, be sure to follow the manufacturer's instructions regarding spacing from walls and ceiling and especially the thru-deck passage for the stove pipe. Secure mounting is also important to keep the stove from shifting as the boat heels. Solid fuel stoves installed aboard boats must meet the provisions of ABYC (American Boat & yacht Council) Standard A-7, Liquid and Solid Fuel Boat Heating Systems and the National Fire Prevention Association Standard #302, Fire Protection Standards for Pleasure and Commercial Motor Craft 1998 Edition.

There is no question that using a solid fuel stove aboard a small boat is more work than just about any other type of stove. All that is mitigated when you can sit back in the cabin on a cold winter's night and watch the flames dancing in your stove. You will have to do a little searching for such a stove, though. Look in the back of specialist and traditional boating magazines for the few suppliers out there.

Another, and very popular, type of solid fuel stove is the charcoal grill. These come in a variety of sizes and shapes. Some are designed to be attached to a stern rail or other mounting system. Others are portable and designed to be used ashore at a picnic or beach party.

I carried one of these inexpensive portable grills on Ternabout for years, first charcoal and later propane. We would beach the boat in a sandy cove and grill lunch on the shore. By the time we had finished lunch and swam for a while the grill had cooled enough to store back aboard. It was much less trouble than it sounds and brings back many happy memories.

Chapter 2: Cooking Fuels and Stoves

Marine grills abound in every boating store and at various price levels. Spend some time investigating and deciding on a mounting system before buying one. Some are designed to mount directly on the stern rail. Others fit accessory mounts that will need to be installed separately. Most are installed so that the charcoal can be dumped directly into the water in case of a fire or flare up. Also be aware that many marinas do not allow charcoal boat grills be used in their slips.

I recently came across another type of solid fuel stove, the Kelly Kettle. These stoves are not for use aboard a boat, rather they are used ashore when camping ashore or picnicking. They can be fueled with just about any readily available solid fuel; sticks, leaves, pine cones, tree bark, dry grass and the like.

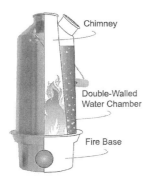 

Figure 11: Diagram of the Kelly Kettle (left) and one in use (right).

A fire pit/base is used to contain the fire. A cylindrical kettle with a central chimney fits on top of the base and directs the heat from the fire up through the kettle. It will boil water in less than 10 minutes. The smallest

29

model will boil a half liter of water in three to five minutes.

Additional accessories will allow the Kelly Kettle to be used to cook meals in addition to boiling water. You can see an online video of these units in operation at www.kellykettleusa.com. They can also be purchased online at www.smallcraftadvisor.com.

Combination Stoves

There are a small number of marine stoves designed as combination units. These utilize shore power for electric heating elements (usually 120 VAC) while at the dock and alcohol burners for use while away from shore power. Most are designed as drop-in units intended to be permanently installed. They are designed for marine service and priced accordingly. A two burner combo stove will run you around $500, a pricey choice. Since most of us don't have dedicated shore power systems or necessarily use marina slips, you'll see few of these stoves aboard our small boats. They are quite common on mid-range power boats with cuddy cabins.

Kerosene and other Liquid Fuel Stoves

Kerosene or diesel fueled stoves are commonplace aboard fishing vessels and larger recreational vessels, especially those used in colder climates. These stoves are designed for permanent installation and make sense when used aboard a vessel that already uses diesel for the propulsion engine (most stoves will burn either diesel or kerosene). Both fuels are widely available, relatively cheap and produce lots of heat.

However, many people object to the smell of diesel or kerosene aboard a boat, saying it hastens the onset of sea-sickness. Great care must be taken in using and refueling such stoves to keep those fumes at bay. They are not a good choice for use aboard a small boat.

Figure 12: A combination kerosene stove/heater. (photo courtesy of Wallas)

Another popular stove, at least in the camping environment, is the ubiquitous green Coleman white gasoline camp stove. (White gas is usually naphtha but can also be pure gasoline without any additives and no smell.) These are similar to pressurized alcohol stoves in that they have a small fuel tank with a built-in pressure pump. Once the tank pressure is built up, the burner knob is cracked open and the burner lit. The liquid white gasoline passes over the flame and is vaporized before being burned in the burner.

While these have proven their worth in decades of outdoor camping, they are not recommended for use aboard a boat. The thought of a pressurized tank of gasoline springing a leak and spraying flaming gasoline throughout the cabin is a scene not to be experienced. Leave this type of stove at home or at camp.

Fire Extinguishers

Regardless of the type of cooking fuel you use, you need to have ready access to fir extinguishers. First of all, it is required equipment if you have an engine. Secondly, it is just good common sense. I have two extinguishers aboard Ternabout. One is installed in the galley area. The other is mounted on a bulkhead a distance from the first. That should ensure that I can get to one or the other in case of a fire.

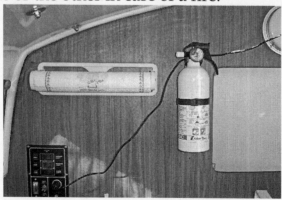

Figure 13: The first fire extinguisher aboard Ternabout. This one is in the galley.

Chapter 2: Cooking Fuels and Stoves

Figure 14: One of two fire extinguishers aboard Ternabout, This one is mounted away from the galley in case of a fire there.

Dry chemical extinguishers are the most common type used aboard our boats. They are equipped with a gauge to verify that there is proper pressure in the extinguisher. Check it often and replace it if it falls outside the green area. In addition, the dry powder inside the extinguisher has a tendency to cake. Remove the extinguisher from the mount and shake it from time to time to make sure the powder is free-flowing.

The Coast Guard Auxiliary, the Power Squadrons and many yacht clubs hold fire safety demonstrations. It is a good idea to attend one if you can. They demonstrate the proper use of fire extinguishers on actual fires and, sometimes, allow attendees to operate the extinguishers. Better to learn how at your leisure than during an actual fire.

Chapter 3: Utensils and Tools

Cooking aboard a small boat, any boat really, requires a certain amount of hardware. The trick is to choose, due to storage constraints, the least amount of hardware to effectively get the job done. On Ternabout, I have a Tupperware utensil container devoted to the majority of the tools discussed in this section.

Knives

Since I'm generally not preparing huge amounts of fresh produce or carving large pieces of meat, I get by with two or three knives. I like a paring knife with a 3-1/2" or 4" blade and a longer serrated knife. I usually have a 6" knife in the container but don't use it often. The knives must be sharp; I take them home from time to time and use a sharpening stone or steel on them.

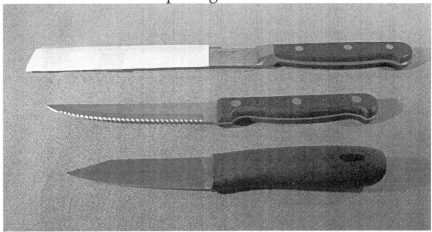

Figure 15: Ternabout's complement of knives. Six inch at top, serrated in the middle and the paring knife at the bottom. Note the protector sleeve on the top knife.

Since they are stored in the utensil container, protecting the blade is a must, otherwise they dull quickly. I usually have a cardboard sleeve protector on each blade. I make these myself from heavy card stock and tape. If I lose one, I'll wrap the blade in a section of paper towel. Either way, I want the cutting edges protected and my fingers safe from cuts when I'm rummaging around in the utensil container.

I like knives with substantial rubber handles for a firm, no-slip, and grip.

Can Openers

Despite the proliferation of pop-top cans, there are still many cans requiring a can opener, I prefer a simple hand operated one with the built in hook for opening bottle caps. Stainless steel is nice if you can find one, but my steel one has lasted years without rusting.

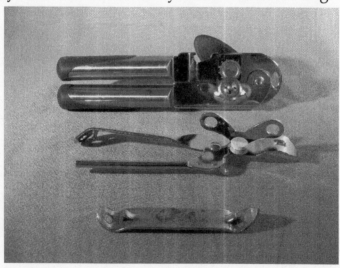

Figure 16: Heavy duty can opener at top, combination can opener/church key in the middle and an old-fashioned church key at the bottom.

Be sure to keep the cutting wheel clean, I've seen some pretty disgusting ones where they haven't been cleaned in years. It, too, resides in the utensil container.

It wouldn't hurt to carry one of those smaller, can-only openers as a spare. You never know when you might drop the main can opener over the side.

No discussion about can openers would be complete without talking about "church keys". This little rascal is getting a little harder to find since the advent of the pop-top can. "Back in the day" it was used to open certain canned beverage containers. It still comes in handy for opening cans of broth and other liquids – or when those pop-top tabs break off. It is a multi-tasking tool in that you can also use the pointed end to widen gelcoat cracks prior to patching them – but that's another book.

Spatulas

I get by with two spatulas. One is a small, flexible, silicon rubber spatula. It's great for scraping out the insides of cans and getting into the corners of my cooking pan. It is small enough to fit inside the utensil container.

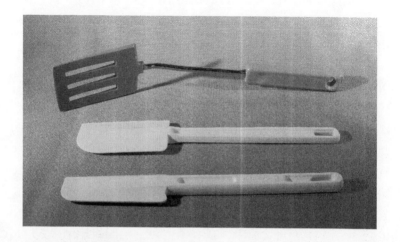

Figure 17: The three spatulas I carry aboard Ternabout. All are non-stick to avoid scratching my non-stick pans.

The second one is a longer handled, pancake, flipper style spatula. It also has a silicone head that won't scratch non-stick pans. Unfortunately, it is too big to fit inside the utensil container so it gets thrown inside the galley box.

Cutlery

While some prefer using plastic cutlery they can throw away after use, I prefer eating with real cutlery. I like a very simple stainless steel design with no fancy work on the handles, just plain flatware. I make do with a knife, fork and spoon for each person. That usually means a maximum of four sets aboard Ternabout.

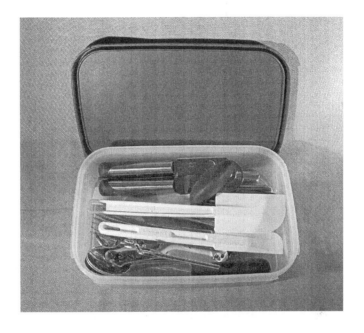

Figure 18: The cutlery resides in the Tupperware utensil container, along with other galley hardware.

In addition, I carry two larger serving spoons for dishing out food. The lack of fancy designs makes them easier to clean and they all fit inside the utensil container.

By the way, that container ends up with a lot of utensils in it. I wrap a lot of them in paper towels just to minimize the rattling sounds when the waves pick up.

39

Dishes

Here again, many use paper plates and bowls and throw them away after use. On a small boat this creates a real trash problem if you are out for any length of time. Aboard Ternabout, we use Melmac plates, cups and bowls. One set per person. The Melmac is tough and easy to clean. These all fit inside the galley box for storage.

Figure 19: I carry four sets of dishes, all that I can comfortably seat on Ternabout.

If you happen to sail in rougher than average seas, you might consider another option in place of bowls and plates: dog dishes. Sounds gross but the wider base of a dog dish means fewer spills and a more stable eating environment. Just don't steal Fido's, get your own new ones.

Figure 20: A heavy-weather, multi-purpose serving dish (Okay, it's a dog dish, but the dog never touched it!)

Pots and Pans

I get by with two pots and pans; a deep saucepan and a frying pan. Both are non-stick, hence the need for special spatulas. I prefer a deep saucepan over a cooking pot because of the built in handle on the saucepan.

Figure 21: I carry a frying pan and a saucepan with lid as my main cooking pots and pans.

Trying to grab the ire bail of a hot cooking pot is hard to do and I think you have less control over the pot compared to a saucepan. If you are going to cook boil-in-the-bag food, it needs to be big enough to hold the cooking water plus the bag.

I've tried several different frying pans and now use one with a fairly high edge to keep contents in the pan and off the stove. Ideally, I would like a square non-stick pan properly sized to fit the stove. I tried a square grill pan once but have since stopped using it. It cooked fine, but trying to fry an egg on the corrugated bottom of the grill pan was an exercise in frustration.

Both the pot and pan store inside the galley box.

Mixing Bowls

The galley box also holds a couple of stainless steel mixing bowls. I don't use them very often but when I need them they are there. Being stainless steel, they won't break and are easy to clean.

Figure 22: Mixing bowls; I don't use them a lot but they are great when I need them.

Coffee/Tea Pot

I drink tea, not coffee but I carry and use a small camping style coffee pot. When not being used to heat tea water, I use it to preheat thermos bottles and washing water. I use instant coffee if I have a coffee drinker on board, I don't like the taste of tea water heated in a pot used to brew coffee.

Fire Starters

No matter what kind of stove you have abroad, it's totally useless unless you have some way of lighting it. I carry two gas grill style lighters aboard. Two because it is hard to tell when one is about to run out of fuel. That usually happens when you are most looking forward to a warm meal or a warm drink. They are also stored in the utensil container.

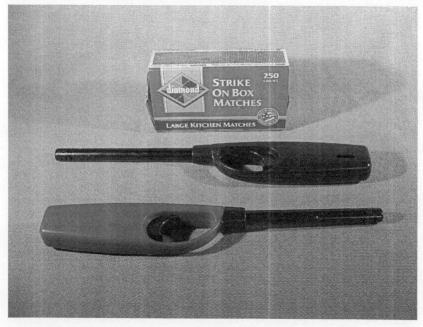

Figure 23: A stove isn't any use unless you have a way of lighting it!

Being a belt-and-suspenders kind of guy, I also carry a box of wooded matches, too. They are stored in their own little waterproof Tupperware container, just in case.

Chapter 3: Utensils and Tools

Thermos Bottles

The common thermos or vacuum bottle can be a very useful cooking tool aboard a small boat. Food can be placed in a pre-heated thermos and left to cook all day, sort of like an unpowered crockpot. Oatmeal, rice and pasta are good candidates for thermos cooking. Soup mixes and Raman noodles are also good choices. So it's not just for your kid's lunch time milk any more. Thermos bottles work by containing a vacuum between an inner flask and an outer liner. The vacuum, being an excellent insulator, retains heat or cold inside the flask.

Figure 24: My Stanley wide-mouth stainless steel thermos. Bulletproof!

The most versatile thermos for use aboard a small boat is a wide mouth version, allowing contents to be easily filled and spooned out. I prefer stainless steel models as they won't shatter like the glass ones when you inevitably drop them. A good stainless steel model will run you around $20. Sizes range from around 14 oz. up to 28 oz. Prices start as low as $15 and go up to almost $50, depending on size and quality. Look for them at Wal-Mart or Kmart; they'll be cheaper there than in a camping store. Match the size of the thermos to the size of the crew. A large thermos, partially filled, is less efficient at cooking and conserving heat than a smaller one completely filled.

As noted in the photo, I purchased a Stanley thermos. As it turned out, I discovered after the purchase that the Stanley was poorly rated as far as heat or cold retention are concerned. So, rest assured, if my recipe worked in the Stanley, it should work in yours. For detailed information of thermos bottle selection visit the theboatgalley.com/ website.

Begin the cooking process by filling the empty thermos with water. Pour that water into a saucepan and bring it to a rolling boil. Pour the boiling water back into the thermos to preheat it. Follow the directions in the recipe you are using. Some call for preheating the contents while others simply have you add the

contents to the now warm thermos. A wide-mouth or canning funnel will make pouring the food to be cooked into the thermos much easier. You can find them for around $4.

Figure 25: A Canning funnel makes filling the thermos much less messy.

47

Cap the thermos and
give it a shake to mix the contents. A slender, long handled spoon, such as an ice tea spoon, helps in getting the last little bit out of the thermos.

Then leave it sit until you are ready to serve. Don't open before then to check the progress! You will lose heat and compromise the cooking process. Check the Recipes chapter for specific thermos cookery recipes. As always, practice these recipes at home before using them on the boat. Anchored in some remote spot is no time to discover a basic flaw in your recipe or technique.

Pressure Cookers

If you have room to store one aboard, a pressure cooker is also a useful cooking tool. A pressure cooker will cook food faster than a conventional pot, thus saving stove fuel. They are available in a wide range of sizes and in either aluminum or stainless steel. You'll pay a premium price for stainless steel but I consider the expense worth it. For example, a 4 quart aluminum pressure cooker will run around $29 while the same size stainless steel one will cost around $47.

Try and pick a size consistent with the amount of cooking you do on the boat. An overly large pressure cooker will waste fuel while a too small one risks overflowing. I recommend waiting until you have accumulated some on-board cooking experience before spending the money on a pressure cooker. It doesn't hurt to use one at home to see if you will even use one aboard. Pay close attention to the pressure cooker recipes, especially the quantities and pressure cooker sizes. Some foods have a tendency to foam when in a pressure cooker and could clog the pressure regulator.

Without the weight on the pressure regulator, a pressure cooker can also be used as a small oven for baking bread. Refer to Chapter 7: Recipes for specific recipes and instructions.

Coolers

From the hot to the cold, I use a couple of coolers aboard Ternabout. There are different sizes to fit different areas of the boat. I started out with a single large Igloo cooler but soon sold it. Not because anything was wrong with the cooler, it just didn't fit the boat or my usage patterns. I prefer two smaller coolers.

One is used for the frozen foods and is usually only opened once a day to get that day's food out. Limiting access to this cooler lengthens the life of the frozen items and the ice. The second cooler holds most of the drinks and the stuff that needs to be kept cool but not ice cold. This cooler is opened often, for beverages, fruit snacks, etc.

I save my small bottled water bottles, refill and then freeze them for use in the coolers. This gives me a ready supply of cold drinking water and reduces the water sloshing around in the cooler. The other thing I did to both coolers was to install a drain plug as low down in each cooler as possible.

D-I-Y Cooler Drain Plug

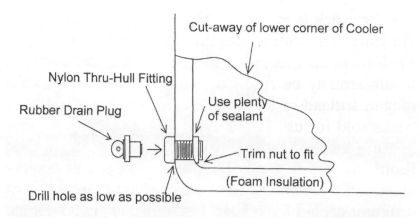

Cut-away of lower corner of Cooler

Nylon Thru-Hull Fitting

Rubber Drain Plug

Use plenty of sealant

Trim nut to fit

(Foam Insulation)

Drill hole as low as possible

This is easily retrofitted using a small through-hull and a rubber drain plug to fit. Simply drill the appropriate sized hole in the side of the cooler and screw the through-hull in place using liberal amounts of a good sealant. This plug allows you to drain any water out of the cooler without having to unload it or tip it. After the water bottles thaw, I switch to ice cubes.

All coolers are not the same. Most are rotationally molded plastic but they vary greatly in terms of the amount of insulation in the cooler walls. Don't overlook the cooler lid, either. It is just as important to have a well-insulated lid as it is the sides. Unfortunately, most molded plastic cooler lids are hollow, not insulated. Keep the cooler out of direct sunlight and cover it with a blanket or towels for insulation. Another useful trick in keeping a cooler cool is to place Styrofoam insulation panels inside, filling up any empty space. It is also important to keep any melted ice water drained from the cooler.

Another trick is to pre-cool the cooler before filling it. Fill the cooler with ice at home before actually placing the food in the cooler. Dump the ice and fill the cooler, it will already be cold and you will keep things cold longer. Instead of ice, you can also use the plastic ice packs sold for use in coolers. They contain a chemical mixture that will actually absorb more heat (and thus cool better) than an equilibrant wright of ice. A well-insulated cooler can be expected to keep things properly cooled for up to five of six days in 90 degree temperatures. Just don't open them often!

Cleaning Supplies

Unfortunately, cooking aboard also means having to clean up aboard. I use paper towels for most clean-up tasks. Store extra rolls in plastic bags to keep them dry. I don't use scouring pads for two reasons; First of all, the steel pads rust and the bronze pads are expensive. Secondly, my cooking pots and pans are non-stick and don't take kindly to be scoured out with a pad. If I burn something in the pan, I first boil water in the pan to loosen up the burnt offering. In extreme cases, I've actually tied a line to a pot or pan and dangled it over the side overnight to loosen things up. Then I boil it out for a final cleaning and sanitizing. I'm not advocating dumping waste food over the side; I'm just soaking the pan so I can get it clean.

I carry a small bottle of dishwashing soap on Ternabout. I try not to use it in excess as I don't like dumping the suds over the side. Packets of wet wipes are handy for cleaning hands and faces after a meal. I use the small coffee pot and/or the saucepan to heat water for washing up. I carry a small plastic dishpan under the sink for use in washing dishes. It's important to use plenty of hot water in order to sanitize the dishes and cooking utensils.

Miscellaneous

I always carry one or two hot pads aboard. They are handy for holding and picking up hot pans or pots. They also do double duty as trivets for placing the hot pots and pans on.

Chapter 3: Utensils and Tools

I've also just started carrying a couple of different sizes of those small plastic flexible cutting boards. There are easy on the knives, easy to clean and can be rolled up like a funnel if need be.

If you are the kind of cook that follows recipes religiously instead of adding ingredients by the "seat-ot-your-pants", you'll need some measuring tools. Some carry a one cup Pyrex measuring cup, although I've never needed one. More important is a set of measuring spoons with various sizes of teaspoons and tablespoons. The set I use are all hooked together with a ring through the handles. That keeps them together and in one place rather than scattered about the utensil container. Stainless steel is good if you can find them and long handles are better than short handled ones.

One final tool that I'll be mentioning several places in this book is the Seal-a-Meal unit. For those of you that have never seen or used one, it is a system of ffood bags and a heat sealing unit. The food is place in the bag and the top closed using the heat sealing feature. The bags are food safe in boiling water, so the contents can be reheated by simply placing them in a pan of boiling water.

When doing your normal cooking at home, you can cook extra and seal them in the bag and freeze them. The frozen bags of food also help keep the cooler cold. I've used these bags for everything from spaghetti sauce, stews, filled crepes, rice and all sorts of recooked pasta.

Pull out a bag of sauce and a bag of cooked spaghetti and place both in the same pot to reheat. In a short while, you have a home-cooked meal ready with almost no prep time and very little mess.

Don't be tempted to use regular Ziploc bags for this purpose. The manufacturer specifically states that the bags have not been tested or approved for "boil in the bag" use.

Chapter 4: Organization

A small boat means small storage and work space. That makes proper and efficient organization all the more important. You need to maximize the work spaces as well as storage spaces or cooking (and staying) aboard becomes an unpleasant chore rather than an enjoyable getaway.

One of the first projects I undertook aboard Ternabout was converting the almost useless cabin table into a cockpit table. If you only do one project aboard your boat, do this one. Its usefulness far outweighs the effort involved.

For years, I used a couple of plastic milk crates to store all the galley equipment and most of the food supplies onboard. I finally got tired of shuffling them around and designed a dedicated galley box. While Ternabout has a small galley area with a useless and small built in cooler (I moved the battery there) and a small sink we don't use. A plastic wash pan lives out in one of the stern lockers and serves as the dishpan.

Another important storage strategy is the use of properly sized plastic storage bins. They are available in a wide variety of sizes and shapes. I spent a fair amount of time optimizing each stage bin for the intended use and available space,

Trash and waste handling becomes an important issue if you camp-cruise away from the dock any length of time. Larger boats are required, by the United States

Coast Guard, to have a trash management plan posted in the galley area. Boats less than 26' aren't required to have such a plan but, believe me; it helps to have worked out all the details before your cruise.

The final section of this chapter deals with Tupperware (and Rubbermaid) containers. I use a host of them aboard Ternabout to organize everything from foods to spare parts. They're easy to find, relatively inexpensive and waterproof, ideal for use aboard a boat.

Cockpit Table

Picture this: you drift into your favorite cove on a dying afternoon breeze. Dropping a stern anchor, you drift up to a tree on the nearby shore. Passing a line around the tree, you pull in the stern anchor line and tuck yourself neatly offshore, away from the bugs (that's the way I did it down in Tennessee). As the sun sets behind the nearby mountain, you prepare an evening meal for your favorite boat companion.

And there you sit, trying to cook, serve and eat your meal while balancing your plate and utensils on your lap, the cockpit seats or any other flat surface within reach. Sound familiar? Well, this upgrade will help solve those problems – a cockpit table.

Ternabout came with a table that was supposed to be used in the cabin. It fit in a recess in the inside of the foot well on the aft end and rested on the galley top of the forward end. The problem was that, with the table in place, you couldn't move in or out of the cabin. I soon made a new, narrower table for the main cabin.

The old table was neat, though. It stored handily under the foot well inside the cabin. A little thought and a few supplies allowed me to turn it into an ideal cockpit table. No more balancing plates on my lap! While you may not have such a table aboard your boat, I'll give you enough information to build your own. In fact, I'll assume you don't have one and go from there. This project assumes you do have a tiller though.

The table itself is a piece of ¾" plywood, 22 x 22 inches. There are several alternatives for this plywood. If you want to be fancy, order up a piece of teak plywood (after taking out the bank loan). You could use a piece of fir plywood, as long as it's not warped and is exterior grade. Any voids should be filled with epoxy. If you can't find flat ¾" plywood, you could take two pieces of 3/8" plywood and epoxy them back-to-back to cancel out any warps.

My choice would be ¾" MDO plywood. This is exterior plywood with a smooth phenolic paper bonded to both sides. It's made with waterproof glue and designed for exterior signs – great stuff and reasonably priced. Contact a local sign shop and see if they'll cut you a piece to the size needed. Note that my table came with a notch in one end to fit around the dagger board trunk. It turned out to be just the thing to provide space for the mainsheet.

Next, you apply an edging and cover the top surface with a laminate (unless you bought the teak-faced plywood). The edging can be any complimentary wood; oak is nice or maybe mahogany. You may also want to cut the corners at a 45° angle, or round them, to avoid sharp, rib attacking corners. Epoxy the strips in place and then sand the top surface smooth. If you are using fir plywood, you will need to seal the wood before applying the laminate. I'd recommend going ahead and coating the whole table with epoxy and sanding smooth.

Once this is done, you can glue the laminate in place with contact cement. I always use the old-fashioned, smelly stuff; it sticks better and lasts longer. Apply two coats to each surface allowing each coat to dry until your finger doesn't stick to it. Place several dowels across the tabletop to support the laminate away from the contact cement while you locate the laminate (you get exactly one chance to get the laminate in the right position, once the two coated surfaces touch, they won't come apart).

Once the laminate is in position, take the center dowel out and press the laminate in place. Work from the center out, removing a dowel and pressing the laminate down. As a final step, use a laminate roller and roll the laminate firmly in place.

With the laminate installed, you can trim the edges with a router and a laminate trimmer bit. If you want to get fancy, you can use an ogee or other bit to form a more complex edge. Or you can just contact cement strips of the same laminate as the top along the sides and then trim the edges to size.

With the tabletop finished, let's move on to the mounting hardware. I cut out a folding aft leg from a piece of ¾" ply. The top end was cut at an angle so the leg would go over center when folded out. You'll need to experiment with the length of the legs to get the table level. The leg unit was fastened to the bottom of the table with a length of piano hinge. I used plastic furniture protectors hammered into the bottom of each leg to protect the fiberglass.

Figure 27: The cockpit table set up with the rear leg folded down and bungeed off to the stern pulpit.

The forward end of the table is held in place by a bracket that fits over the end of the tiller. Ternabout's tiller is square, which worked out great. The tiller is clamped in place by a short length of wood and tightened with two wing nuts. The wing nuts turn on two hanger bolts screwed into the brace. If you measure properly the first time, you won't have to add the spacer to the brace that I did on my table.

Figure 28: A view from below showing the forward tiller mount.

Figure 29: The folding rear leg stowed and bungeed in place.

I also screwed eyebolts into the aft side of the brace and the leg. I used a short bungee cord to keep the leg folded flat while stored. When I'm ready to deploy the table, I set the tiller tamer to hold the tiller in place. Then it is a simple matter to unfold the legs and clamp the forward bracket on the end of the tiller. The bungee goes around the mainsheet horse and the eyebolt in the table leg to hold the aft end of the table steady.

The table stores under the cockpit foot well on the inside of the cabin. An "L" shaped runner is fastened to each side of the lower surface of the foot well to allow the table to freely slide in and out. It never slides out while under way, probably because there is too much other junk in the way.

Well, now you can enjoy that quiet evening in your favorite cove, just you and your whoever. Well, except for those 200hp, 16' bass boats – but dealing with them is a whole 'nother project!

Cockpit Table Side View

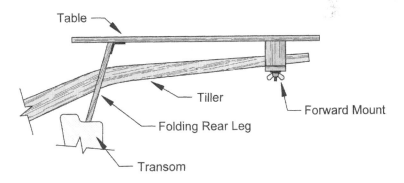

Table

Tiller

Forward Mount

Folding Rear Leg

Transom

Aft End of Cockpit Table

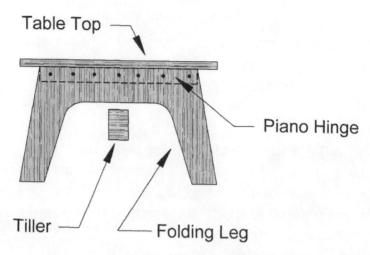

Table Top

Piano Hinge

Tiller

Folding Leg

Forward End of Table

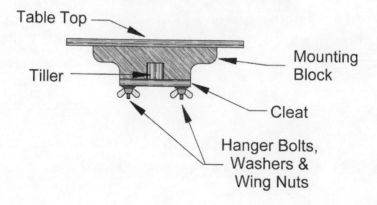

Table Top

Tiller

Mounting Block

Cleat

Hanger Bolts, Washers & Wing Nuts

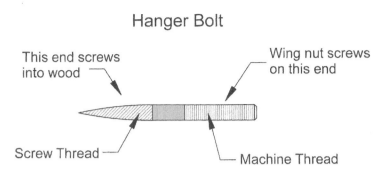

Hanger Bolt

This end screws into wood

Wing nut screws on this end

Screw Thread

Machine Thread

Galley Box

Many smaller boats, power or sail, do not have a dedicated galley area. Yet many of these boats are used for boating camping or extended overnight trips. One answer to this problem is a custom gallery box.

I had been spending many weekends and long holidays aboard Ternabout. There was a rudimentary galley area but it was totally unusable. The idea of lighting a stove and cooking below, especially in a hot Tennessee summer, was ridiculous. Yet I enjoyed cooking aboard and most of all, eating well while afloat.

So I carried my galley gear aboard in a collection of plastic crates and boxes, stacked wherever I could find room in the cabin. I cooked, using my trusty and slightly rusty Coleman propane two burner camping stove. Life was not perfect, though. It seemed the utensil or dish I needed was always in the bottom of the back plastic crate, buried under other equipment.

I had seen several examples of camping or galley boxes in the past but couldn't find one that met my needs and space. So I decided to research and build a custom galley box.

As in any project, preparation is key and this project was no different. I started by rounding up all the bits and pieces I wanted to house in my galley box so I could document the spaces required. Many of the galley boxes I had seen were huge and too large to comfortably move aboard or store. I would be moving the box from the cabin out into the cockpit for use and so wanted the smallest possible box that would hold the required gear.

After sorting through that gear, I decided that the box would need to hold the following:

- The Coleman stove (the cylinders were already stowed outside on the stern rail)
- A cutlery box with flatware, knives, can opener and other small utensils
- A spice box for my collection of spices and staples like sugar
- Place settings for four, small plates, mugs and bowls
- A large and a small frying pan
- A coffee (in my case tea) pot for boiling water.
- One or more small pots

I still wasn't totally convinced my plan was workable so I decided to build a quick and dirty prototype out of artists foam board. It's made from a sheet of plastic foam sandwiched between two sheets of card stock. I use this stuff for a host of different projects, templates and patterns. It's cheap, especially if you look for sales, easy to cut and can be glued and taped together into quite a sturdy piece. Not strong or weather proof enough for a final item but certainly strong enough to try out, move it around and place all the gear in it.

My first step was to gather the gear together and measure each piece or set to be stored. In my case, I then transferred these dimensions to my computer drawing program and juggled them around for the best fit. Lacking such a program, it would make sense to make a paper cutout of the items and then move them around for the best fit.

With the design completed, I then started laying out the parts on the foam board. I used ½″ stock for the bottom, top and ends and 3/16″ stock for all other pieces. I use an X-Acto knife with a #11 blade and a steel ruler to make all the cuts. For better accuracy, I mark both sides and cut partially through from each side. A quick snap pops the center foam for a clean and accurate cut.

I use wide blue masking tape to hold the parts together while the glue dries. The tape can be peeled away from the board without tearing the surface. My glue of choice is either Elmer's white glue or Titebond II; both work well with the foam board.

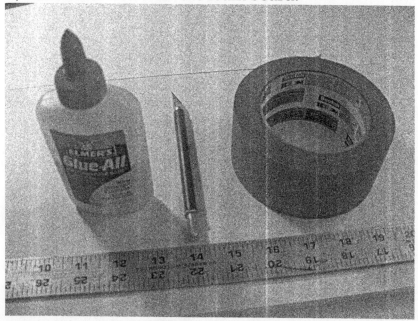

Figure 30: The essential tools for building a foam board mock-up.

As you can see from the pictures and drawings, the stove is carried on top of the galley box, bungeed in place. I wanted some extra working space so I designed the front of the box to fold down with chain or light line to keep it level. On the real box, I'm planning of using a piece of ½" StarBoard so I can also use it as a cutting board. The StarBoard will add a little weight but the added utility of a cutting board is well worth it.

The prototype went together over the course of several days. The longest delay was simply waiting for the glue joints to dry. Once completed, I loading it and all the gear and took them out to the boat for trials. While the overall design concept worked well, there were some details that needed changed or improved upon.

Initially, the shelves were open and the items simply stacked in the openings. However, when I went to open the front of the box after moving it out into the cockpit, I found the contents falling out. I added a strip of 3/8" square stock to the front edge of each compartment as a lip to hold things in place. That solved that problem. The bottom of the final box would also require nonskid, non-scratching bumpers on the bottom.

The other major problem was an oversight on my part; I didn't put handles on the box. The final product would need adequately sized handles on each end to make moving the box around practical, a simple fix.

Now that I'm happy with the prototype, I can move on to making the real thing. I've decided on using marine plywood for all but the front of the box. The top, bottom and ends as well as the center vertical divider will be 3/8" Okoume plywood. The shelves and back will be ¼" Okoume. The shelves will be epoxied into shallow rabbets (grooves) in the 3/8" ply. The whole box will be well sealed with several coats of epoxy for durability.

I strongly recommend making a prototype like this for any major boat projects. It's much easier to make a mistake or do a redesign with a couple of buck's worth of foam board, tape and glue. I'll be honest, some prototypes I've built turned out to be real duds, and I would have hated to spend all that time and money on expensive plywood and glue. Nothing beats trying out the full sized item in its intended place.

Front View of Galley Box

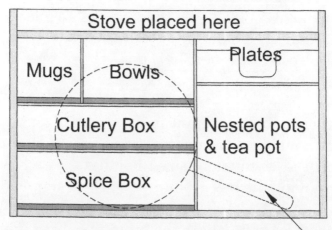

Frying pans in front of shelves

Side View of Galley Box

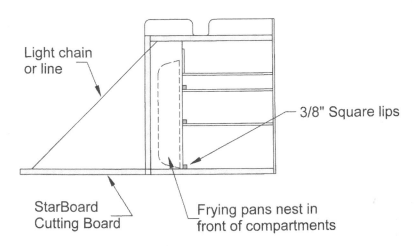

Light chain
or line

3/8" Square lips

StarBoard
Cutting Board

Frying pans nest in
front of compartments

Plywood Construction Details

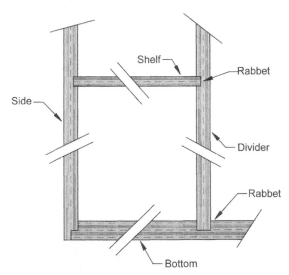

Shelf

Rabbet

Side

Divider

Rabbet

Bottom

Cooking Aboard a Small Boat

Figure 31: The galley box closed up.

Figure 32: The galley box with the StarBoard cutting board lowered.

Figure 33: Another view of the galley box and its contents.

Storage Boxes & Stowage Spaces

Storage space aboard is always at a premium and food storage is no different. Ternabout nominally sleeps four but I decided to use the two quarter berths for storage. Canned goods go into plastic tubs with tight sealing tops. The cans lie on their sides and are stacked about two rows deep. If you read cruising books from "back in the day", cruisers spent hours peeling off labels, writing the can contents on the cans and then varnishing the cans to protect them from corrosion. A properly sized (long and narrow) storage box will keep canned goods neat, organized and dry, even with the labels on.

Figure 34: One of the can storage boxes. More and smaller boxes are easier to carry and stow than fewer but larger boxes.

Most of these storage boxes are not Tupperware of RubberMaid as I haven't found the right sizes in those products. The lids are not nearly as waterproof as Tupperware of RubberMaid brand, so I'm careful where I store them. Most reside on top of the port quarterberth.

The storage area under the starboard quarterberth is devoted to drinks. A combination of sodas, bottled water and juices are all stored on their sides up against the bottom of the boat. This is usually the coolest part of the boat in the summer. When I was in Tennessee, the lake I was on never froze in the winter and the warmer water kept the drinks from freezing even when the outside air temperature (rarely) dropped below freezing.

Before I built a galley box, the rest of my galley supplies were kept in two plastic milk crates. One contained all the accessories, pots, pans, silverware and other utensils (in a sealed Tupperware container), as well as paper towels, trash bags, Ziploc bags, stove lighters and such.

The other crate held (and still does) my dry ingredients, tea, sugar, sweetener, the spice box, oatmeal, dry sauce mixes, instant soups and noodles, raisins, nuts and similar foods. I usually keep this crate at home and take it out to the boat when needed. That way I know what's there and what needs replaced.

Figure 35: This blue plastic crate holds the oversize gear that dosen't fit elsewhere.

The crates are fairly light and can easily be moved where necessary, in or out of the cabin. Normally, they are bungeed in front of the galley counter.

Matilda's have a rudimentary galley on the port side, up against the vee-berth bulkhead. This consists of a small icebox and a small sink with a storage locker below, next to the daggerboard case. The icebox will barely hold a six-pack and a small amount of ice and the sink wasn't much better. I had moved the battery box up into the icebox space to be close to the new electrical panel and help the weight distribution.

Figure 36: The miniscule galley area aboard Ternabout now used mainly for storage. Note the black walnut fiddles.

In the end, I cut a piece of three-quarter inch birch plywood to cover the galley area and added a couple of black walnut fiddles to keep stuff in place. I put a screw eye in the vee-berth bulkhead and another in the daggerboard case. The stove is then bungeed vertically using these eyes. The bottom (end) of the stove rests on a piece of Dri-Dek tile.

A fire extinguisher and a paper towel rack are also bolted to the aft side of the vee-berth bulkhead.

Spice Box

One essential item, at least for me, is a decent collection of spices. The addition of spices to dehydrated or canned foods makes all the difference in the world. My spice box is a square plastic Tupperware container that seals well and resides in the galley box.

I use the smaller sizes of spice containers because I use them faster, avoiding stale or old tasting spices. You can also save those packets of silica gel drying agents you sometimes get. Throw a couple in the spice box to reduce humidity and prolong the useful life of your spices.

Figure 37: The spice box, key to great tasting meals.

Just looking through our box, I find the following:

- Oregano
- Chili powder
- Ground Cumin

- Whole dried chilies
- Beef bouillon
- Chicken bouillon

- Salt
- Pepper
- Dried onions
- Garlic powder
- Bay leaf
- Thyme
- Celery flakes
- Dried parsley

- Onion powder
- Cayenne pepper
- Worcestershire sauce
- Frank's Louisiana Hot Sauce (substitute Tabasco or Texas Pete if you must.)

Again, use smaller containers so the spices don't get stale and lose their potency. Your spice box should contain roughly the same spices you use at home. Out on the boat is not really the best place to develop new menu items! Be sure to take any spices or seasonings any special recipe on the menu requires, you might not have it aboard.

Trash Baskets and Waste Disposal

Spending more time away from the dock unfortunately means less access to the dock dumpster. If you aren't careful, the trash from a week's cruising could overwhelm you. Boats over 26-feet are required to have a Marpol Trash Placard aboard, defining what and where garbage can be disposed. Boats over 40 feet must have a written garbage disposal plan aboard. The Marpol international regulations define what and how far offshore it's legal to dispose of certain garbage and trash. Suffice to say, our boats seldom get to a point where it is legal to dump any trash overboard. Besides, do we really want to dump our trash where we swim and fish?

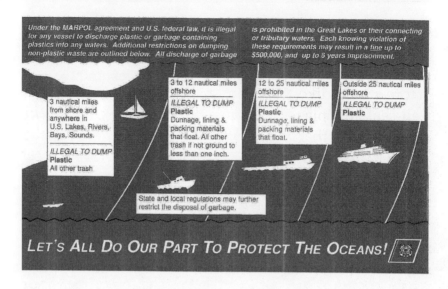

Under the MARPOL agreement and U.S. federal law, it is illegal for any vessel to discharge plastic or garbage containing plastics into any waters. Additional restrictions on dumping non-plastic waste are outlined below. All discharge of garbage is prohibited in the Great Lakes or their connecting or tributary waters. Each knowing violation of these requirements may result in a fine up to $500,000, and up to 6 years imprisonment.

3 nautical miles from shore and anywhere in U.S. Lakes, Rivers, Bays, Sounds.

ILLEGAL TO DUMP
Plastic
All other trash

3 to 12 nautical miles offshore

ILLEGAL TO DUMP
Plastic
Dunnage, lining & packing materials that float. All other trash if not ground to less than one inch.

12 to 25 nautical miles offshore

ILLEGAL TO DUMP
Plastic
Dunnage, lining & packing materials that float.

Outside 25 nautical miles offshore

ILLEGAL TO DUMP
Plastic

State and local regulations may further restrict the disposal of garbage.

LET'S ALL DO OUR PART TO PROTECT THE OCEANS!

Figure 38: The MARPOL trash placard.

So managing trash on board needs to be thought out ahead of time and prepared for. I carry one trash basket aboard Ternabout. A regular flexible plastic wastepaper basket fits neatly alongside the port quarterberth and the cockpit footwell.

An ample supply of heavy-duty white trash bags with draw strings is stashed in the galley. Full trash bags are stowed in one of the cockpit lockers until they can be disposed of properly ashore. Even so, trash storage capacity is limited and must be properly used.

That process begins ashore. I remove as much of the original packing as I can. Discard the cardboard boxes and store the contents in Ziploc bags, Besides, I have a rule – no cardboard allowed onboard. It's not much of a problem up north, but cockroaches often sneak aboard in cardboard packing farther south.

I store staples like sugar, flour, tea bags and the like in well-sealed plastic containers (Tupperware or RubberMaid) that I can refill ashore at the end of the cruise. I prefer canned soft drinks as opposed to plastic bottles as the cans can be crushed to take up less space when empty.

I have a cheap can crusher mounted on a small piece of board. The board has a cleat on each end so the can crusher can be placed on the trash basket without slipping off. Having the can crusher over the trash basket catches any liquids left in the cans being crushed.

Figure 39: The can crusher fits on top of the trash basket to catch any stray drips.

Steel cans usually have both ends opened with a can opener and then are simply flattened to take up less space. Clean the cans thoroughly before crushing to reduce any smell from the trash basket. What few paper boxes that are on board should be carefully broken down and flattened to take up as little space as possible.

I have another useful accessory to go with my trash basket. It's a wooden cutting board I like to use in prepping food. The board has cleats on the bottom so I can place it on the trash basket without danger of it slipping off. A large hole in one corner allows me to push trimmings into the trash basket without moving the cutting board. I usually use it sitting on the starboard quarterberth with it between my knees. That way it is not in any danger from tipping from an errant wave or wake.

Figure 40: The cutting board also sits o top of the trash basket, catching any food scraps.

A word about selecting a cutting board: you can choose from a wide variety of plastic of wood cutting boards, just take a trip through any kitchen store. While it might seem that an inert plastic cutting board might be safer from contamination, tests have proven that hardwood cutting boards are much easier to keep clean than plastic ones. I wipe off the cutting board after each use and pour hot water over it to sanitize it.

Give your trash management plan some thought before leaving the dock, your cruise-mates and the environment will thank you.

Tupperware & RubberMaid

You've probably noticed that I have mentioned using both Tupperware and Rubbermaid containers in many sections of this book. They are a godsend to the small boat sailor. The wide variety of sizes and shapes coupled with their relatively low price and ability to keep their contents dry make them invaluable aboard.

There are a lot of cheaper knock-offs on the market but I've found it best to stick to the proven brands, They keep the contents dry, stay sealed and are quite strong.

I keep my staples (flour, sugar, tea bags and the like) in these containers. Over the years, I've geared the size of the container to the amount of supplies I need to keep on board. Don't be afraid to change the container size as you adapt to cooking aboard, I seldom picked the right size the first time. The good news is that there is always a ready market for these containers at any yard sale.

Figure 41: A few of the Tupperware and RubberMaid containers I use aboard Ternabout.

I also use a variety of these containers to store spare parts onboard. Labeling the top of the container helps in quickly finding what you are looking for. Most of my spare parts containers fit under the port quarterberth and the separate containers keep the parts organized and in perfect condition.

Cooking Aboard a Small Boat

Chapter 5: Preparation

Like any human activity, the devil is in the details. In terms of eating well aboard your small boat, that means spending a little time on preparation. It might seem like a lot of work in the beginning but, as you gain experience, it will become second nature and go quickly.

Menu Planning

The first step in preparing for cooking aboard for any length of time is to prepare a menu. It needn't be exotic; in fact it works better if you pattern it after your regular, at-home menu. The middle of a cruise is no time to try a new menu item, you may not like it! If you are like most of us, you'll need to allow a little more quantity of food than usually consumed at home. Something about being out on the water makes all food taste better regardless of your culinary skills.

The menu should be detailed enough to allow you to gather all the necessary items. I maintain a recipe file on my computer, even for the simplest items. I can then put together an ingredient list and from that, a shopping list, at the drop of a hat. I keep daily menus on my computer also, which simplifies putting together a week or so worth of menus. It is important that each menu list the number of servings it will yield. That will allow you to adjust for differing numbers of crew aboard. Running out of food is frowned on by your crew. As I said, the more you do it, the easier and quicker it becomes.

Once you have the menu in hand, you can gather the necessary supplies for your cruise. Some will come from supplies on hand. For the rest, prepare a shopping list.

Proper menu planning will take into account the types of foods you take on board. For example, the first day or so can be fresh, unfrozen foods. As those food run out you will need to switch to your frozen itens. Once they run out, you need to use your shelf stable items, canned goods and the like.

Shopping

Most of us will do the boat shopping at the same time we do the regular household shopping. That way you can spot the best bargains and minimize separate trips. The one or two special items, including ice, can be picked up at the last minute, perhaps on the way to the boat. If you have freezer space or pantry space, with your list in hand you can pick up larger quantities for future cruises. Base these purchases on proven menus and recipes. As mentioned before, the middle of a week-long cruise is no place to try a new and unproven recipe.

I keep my spice box and plastic crate of staples at home between boating trips so I can check quantities and freshness and replace or refill as necessary.

Preparation

I spend some time preparing my food purchases before the cruise. My first activity is to reduce, as much as possible, the amount of packaging material going aboard. I take things out of boxes and place them in Ziploc baggies. While not a great problem in northern climes, cockroaches and other pests can come aboard in packaging in warmer climates. I try and reduce, as much as possible, the amount of trash I have to dispose of aboard the boat.

If you use a Seal-a-Meal unit and boil-in-the-bag bags, you can do a lot of food preparation in conjunction with your regular home cooking. Just increase the amount being prepared, seal the excess in the bag and freeze. Over the course of a couple weeks or months, you'll build up a supple of boat-ready food that only need to be placed in the cooler.

If you don't have a Seal-a-Meal, Ziploc baggies also work but can't be used as boil-in-the bag bags, the plastic isn't rated for boiling water.

I prepare any fresh vegetables ahead of time. Carrots are peeled, celery cleaned and cut, lettuce washed, dried and all are placed in separate stay-fresh produce bags (Green Bags).

Meats are divided up and bagged according to the menu plan. Each bag contains the meat for a given recipe. Once bagged, they are hard- frozen and so will help keep the cooler cool. I don't like taking raw hamburger aboard, even in a cooler. So I fry the hamburger ahead of time and then portion it out into baggies and then freeze it. It can then be added to spaghetti sauce, goulash, tacos or whatever you need it for.

I also prepackage any dry ingredients for a given recipe. Spices, seasonings, rice or flour can all be placed in a baggie ready for use. Be sure and label these baggies so you know exactly what they contain. Many baggies have a matt area that will allow you to write directly on the bag. Dry bagged items can be labeled with a computer-generated label, but don't forget they aren't waterproof.

The bottom line is to do as much food preparation at home and ahead of time as is practical. The more time spent preparing at home means less time doing it aboard, often under less than ideal conditions.

Chapter 6: Foods and Drinks

Iron Rations

The first category of foods is canned, iron rations if you please. I typically keep a selection of them aboard for the end-of-cruise meals or when I find ourselves staying out longer than expected. The good news is that the variety and quality of canned goods keeps on improving

Every once in a while a boating magazine will run an article touting the durability of Dinty Moore beef stew. Now, I've eaten it on occasion, but it isn't one of my favorites. A little red wine and a lot of spice from the spice box seem to help.

Soups, stews and some great one-pot casseroles can be whipped up from the proper selections of cans. Since I sail the boat year around, I find I make more of these heartier meals, as the season grows colder. Again, don't be shy with the seasonings from your spice box!

I store the cans in plastic boxes stored on top of the starboard quarter berth, pushed all the way aft. We use several boxes to make them a little lighter and easier to handle. Looking through them now, I find some of the following: Great Northern beans, Hormel ham, turkey, chicken, mushrooms, green beans, peas, peaches, pears, fruit cocktail, apple sauce, fruit juices, tomato juice, soups, crushed tomatoes, tomato paste, spaghetti, chili, and Vienna Sausages (a boyhood favorite, don't ask).

Figure 42: Canned meats and seafoods are important "iron rations".

The Hormel canned meats are ideal for use aboard. I combine them with other items to make everything from gumbo, to chicken corn chowder to white chicken chili. If you live in a locale with an Amish or

Mennonite store, check out their canned meats. They have a wide variety and good prices in slightly larger size cans.

There are also online stores, usually purveyors of survival type foods that offer everything from canned butter to canned cheese and canned bacon. They are a little pricey but if you have to have your bacon on a long cruise, it's a viable solution.

Canned soups are a staple aboard Ternabout. The condensed soups store compactly and require an equal amount of water to reconstitute. The cream soups; cream of celery, chicken, mushroom and cheddar cheese, are useful in making one pot meals like stews and casseroles. The Chunky Campbell's and Progresso soups don't require extra water, just heat and eat.

Figure 43: Chopped chilies, sliced mushroom and sliced olives are great flavor enhancers.

I also keep a supply of small cans of mushrooms, sliced black olives and chopped green chilies aboard. These can be added to a wide variety of dishes for extra flavor and texture. To round out my supply of canned foods, I have canned mixed vegetables, green beans, pork and beans, kidney beans as well as a selection of canned tomatoes, tomato paste and tomato sauce.

Here are some things to watch out for with canned goods. First of all, never use a can that's leaking or bulged, a case of botulism could ruin your whole day. Also watch out for canned goods with the pop-top tabs. These cans are usually fine, but the tops are vulnerable and can leak when bumped. Thirdly, I keep canned (evaporated) milk aboard for my tea and for use over canned fruit. For some reason, the small cans I use don't have a very long shelf life so I only stock a can or two and use them often. Another option is a small can of condensed milk. This is thicker than evaporated milk and contains sugar. It works well if you like cream and sugar in your coffee or tea.

Many hard-core cruising books talk of taking the labels off of the cans and writing the contents on the can with an indelible marker. Some even go as far as suggesting you coat the can with varnish to prevent rusting. We don't store any canned goods in the bilge (it's only 2" deep!) so bilge water soaking off the labels isn't a problem. If the can stays aboard long enough to rust, you either have stocked too much, sailed too little or didn't like that selection to begin with.

I avoid bringing aboard any glass jars or containers, I figure if I don't have it aboard, I can't drop it and break it.

Freeze-dried/Instant/Unrefrigerated Foods

As your cruise continues away from readily available ice, other foods will need to be considered. There is a wide range of dehydrated and freeze-dried food available at your local sporting goods or camping store. These foods are usually reconstituted with boiling water. Some of these items are great and others are so-so. Unfortunately, the only way to find out is to try them. Don't be afraid to liberally use the contents of your spice box when appropriate. Mountain House is one popular brand and I really like their Raspberry Crumble dessert.

There are also an increasing number of prepackaged and unrefrigerated (shelf stable) meals available in your local grocery store. These have a fairly long lifetime but are a little bulkier than the dehydrated/freeze dried meals. Some are designed to be rehydrated with boiling water while others are fully hydrated and ready for a microwave.

Figure 44: There is a great variety of shelf-stable complete meals on grocery shelves. Be sure to try them before buying any quantity.

Alternately, they can be heated by immersing them in boiling water, much like a "boil-in-the-bag" pouch. The downside to this is that the instructions call for immersion in boiling water for almost ten minutes. That is a lot of stove time and fuel. Since few of us have a microwave aboard, I've also heated these meals by emptying them into a pan on the stove. It was much quicker than the boiling water method. Same caveat as above. Try 'em BEFORE you leave the dock to make sure you like them as the reviews of some of these products rate them as less than stellar. The one I sampled was a sigle-serving package. It would be okay for a sedentary office worker's lunch, but out on the water you'll need two of them to satisfy your hunger.

Figure 45: Dry seasoning mixes come in a bewildering variety but are great for quick flavor development.

Also available at your grocery store are dry mixes. In addition to any imaginable sauce, gravy or soup, there are main dish items like potatoes au gratin, noodles with various sauces and so on. Throw in a couple to go with the steaks or pork chops. Oh yes, don't forget macaroni and cheese and that perennial favorite, Raman Noodles.

Figure 46: If all else fails, there is always a package of Ramen Noodles around.

Another dry ingredient is something called TVP, Textured Vegetable Protein. This dry, granular product is derived from soy beans and is available in natural, beef, bacon, chicken, taco and ham flavors. I have only used the beef flavored product. I've added it as a thickener and flavoring to soups and stews and in place of hamburger in spaghetti sauce. It is commonly found in your local health food store.

Include any of your favorite snacks. Chips, power bars, candy, pretzels and crackers will take the edge off your hunger while underway. I store mine in Tupperware or RubberMaid containers, they'll stay dry and fresh longer.

Chapter 6: Foods and Drinks

I mentioned canned and condensed milk in the "Iron Rations" section. There is another choice for dairy products, UHT milk. UHT stands for Ultra High Temperature, a preservation method that works so well that milk products can be stored at room temperature for long periods.

According to the Borden's website:
> "UHT stands for Ultra High Temperature pasteurization and packing. Applying this special process produces milk that will be fresh and natural for several months without refrigeration. UHT milk has extended shelf life (shelf stable) and is sometimes called long life or extended life milk also. No preservatives are added. Once the pack has been opened it must be refrigerated. UHT milk is a perfect choice for breakfast, school lunch, hiking, biking, camping, travel, food storage, emergency preparedness, and disaster response."

A variety of different products are available; 1%, 2% and whole milk, chocolate milk and half and half. Best of all it is available in small, 8 oz. containers (you need to use it quickly as it will otherwise need refrigeration).

Figure 47: UHT milk comes in these handy 8 oz. cartons.

Many cheeses can be stored at room temperature; in fact they taste better that way. Hard cheeses last longer and cheese packaged in plastic or a have wax coating will last almost indefinitely. Any small spots of mold that develop after the cheese has been opened can be cut away. Grated parmesan cheese is another cheese product I like to have on board. In addition to using it on spaghetti, you can add to many dishes, including scrambled eggs, stews and soups.

Chapter 6: Foods and Drinks

Peanut butter, jams and jellies, honey and pancake syrup can all be stored at room temperature. I don't often take these along but when I do, I transfer a modest amount to a RubberMaid or Tupperware container. This is because many of these products come in glass jars and I try to avoid having breakable glass containers on board.

No discussion of un-refrigerated food would be complete without mentioning MRE's (Meals – Ready to Eat). Complete, nutritious – Yes. Exciting – No. If you feel there is a chance you may get stranded on a desert island like Tom Hanks, throw a couple in the lazarrette or the bilge, it won't hurt them. Besides, you can always use them to chock the trailer wheels.

Pre-packaged

Since my usual cooking vessels consist of one frying pan and one saucepan, I favor one-pot type entrees. When I'm cooking a one-pot meal at home, I make enough extra for another meal. I then seal it in a plastic boiling bag and freeze it.

You could use plastic containers but I find the bags are easier to store and I don't have the dirty containers left afterward. Don't forget, your cruising plans should include proper provisions for trash disposal.

I also find that I usually have a better appetite aboard so I allow just a little more. Don't overdo it, though, you want to make sure you don't have any leftovers.

You can get as fancy as you want. I've done turkey crepes (turkey and cheese rolled in a crepe) with sauce, pasta items and so forth. Seal the sauce in a separate bag from the crepes or pasta. Boil the bags in the same pan and combine after heating.

Meats should be well-frozen and packed in one meal sized packages. Due to food safety concerns, I usually don't take foods like uncooked hamburger or raw chicken with me. Steaks, bacon, ham and pork chops all freeze well (use boneless cuts, saves on waste).

Cooking bacon on board is a messy affair. There is always the problem of disposing of the bacon grease leftover from frying the bacon. The best method I've found is to precook the bacon beforehand. Place the strips of bacon on a rack over a shallow pan and place in the oven. Bake until crisp. This keeps the bacon strips nice and flat and easy to package. I wrap enough bacon for one meal in aluminum foil and then freeze. I can then warm the bacon up, in the opened foil package, on the stove.

I also prepackage as much of the fresh vegetables and fruit as I can. Again, the intent is to reduce the time spent preparing food aboard as well as reducing the amount of trash and garbage to be properly disposed of ashore. Carrots, celery and radishes can be peeled and cut into sticks and bite size pieces and stored in plastic baggies in the cooler; both for snacks as for including in other dishes.

I also prepackage many of the dry ingredients I will need for specific recipes. For example, I prepackage my morning oatmeal, in individual servings, in Ziploc baggies. This makes locating the item to cook much quicker and also makes sure you have the necessary ingredients on hand for the dish you are preparing. You won't end up finding you don't have enough of an item in your bulk storage midway through preparing the dish. I label each bag with the contents and the date so I use the oldest bag first. Many food storage bags now come with a matt area designed to write on with a marker. If you use computer-generated labels, remember that they aren't waterproof, don't use them on bags that will be frozen or put in the cooler.

Frozen Foods

Frozen food encompasses everything from prepared meals sealed in plastic boiling bags to prepackaged meats and vegetables and everything else in between. Many fruits and vegetables are available in frozen bags, usually in large economy sizes. These can be repacked into meal-sized servings and placed back in your home freezer to freeze solidly. Examples are things like hash browns, mixed vegetables and chopped onions as well as cherries and various berries.

The important thing is to make sure the food is frozen solidly and packaged well. Arrange your menu so that the fresh food is used first, followed by the frozen foods. You should be using two coolers; one with drinks and such that gets opened often and another for frozen food that only gets opened once a day, to get that day's food items out. Properly managed and with a good cooler, you can keep food frozen for up to five or six days.

Some have suggested using dry ice (frozen CO_2) to keep foods frozen longer. While this will work, if you stow your coolers in the same cabin you sleep in, you could be taking your life in your hands. CO_2 sublimates directly into gaseous carbon dioxide. CO_2 gas is heavier than air and could possible displace the oxygen in your cabin. Don't risk it.

An unintended byproduct of using dry ice is that anything not frozen risks being carbonated. I used dry ice in a cooler on a road trip once. By the third day, the jar of pickles in the cooler was thoroughly carbonated. It made for a strange tasting sandwich.

Fresh Foods

Fresh foods can be divided into two groups, refrigerated and unrefrigerated.

Refrigerated Fresh Foods

These foods require some degree of cooling to remain safe to eat. Some examples are unfrozen meats, cold cuts, some fruits and vegetables as well as some baked goods. Since the length of time your ice will keep these items cold may be limited, it is important to plan your menus so as to use these items first.

Unrefrigerated Fresh Foods

These foods require no refrigeration to remain safe and unspoiled. Foods in this category are items like dried salami, peperoni, onions, potatoes, tomatoes, apples, oranges, lemons and eggs. Unrefrigerated eggs, fresh from the farm, last longest. Eggs should be kept in a hard plastic egg container (available at most camping stores) to protect them from breakage. Turn the egg container over every day or so. These foods don't all have an indefinite shelf life but are safe for the length of most cruises.

Condiments & Staples

Additionally, don't forget the dry staples like rice, noodles, pasta, sugar, raisins, tea bags, coffee and flour. I keep them in sealed Tupperware or RubberMaid containers and take only as much as I think I will need for the cruise. The containers are waterproof and keep the contents dry and bug-free.

Pancakes are easy to make with UHT or evaporated milk and cooked in your frying pan with a little cooking spray. I don't often fix pancakes aboard so I prepackage the pancake mix, enough for the current cruise only, to keep it fresh. Use a squeeze bottle for the butter and another one for the syrup.

Cooking rice aboard can be problematic. I'm a rice snob and prefer Basmati rice. It takes longer to prepare than Minute Rice and requires simmering on the stove. This is difficult on many of the stoves we use aboard our boats. So I usually prepare the rice ahead of time and seal it in a bag. Your other option is to use quick cooking Minute Rice, but I don't think the flavor is as good.

Many consider bread a staple but keeping it from getting wet and moldy aboard is a problem. One method is to toast each piece of bread and place it in a baggy. The toasting will dry out the bread and the baggie will keep it dry. By packing each piece individually, you use what you need without opening other baggies. Camping stores sell toaster racks that fit on top of the stove burner to warm and freshen the toast, if you like.

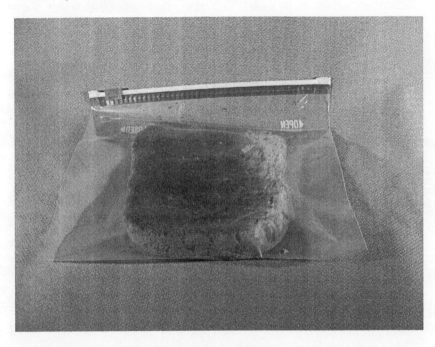

Figure 48: Bread can be toasted then stored in Ziploc bags.

Don't forget instant potatoes flakes. Many brands actually taste as good as real potatoes. They can be used for everything from mashed potatoes, garlic potatoes to soup and stew thickeners. I keep a Tupperware container of them in my staples crate.

Prepackaged condiment envelopes (ketchup, mayonnaise, mustard and the like) are also fine if you don't leave them aboard for too long. Pick up a few extras every time you visit your favorite fast food restaurant.

Many bottles of condiments will last for a long time even when unrefrigerated. Ketchup, mayonnaise, mustard and Frank's Hot Sauce are good examples. Parkay also has their margarine in a squeeze bottle. Always use clean utensils in the jars to avoid any cross contamination. I select small plastic bottles and squeeze containers whenever available. That way, they are used up quicker and will always be fresh.

I also keep a spray can of cooking oil on hand. They are available in a wide range of flavors; from olive oil to butter flavor. It makes frying much less messy, even in non-stick pans. I also carry a small plastic bottle of olive oil for those occasions when a little more oil is appropriate. You could also carry corn oil, vegetable oil, peanut oil or the like if your tastes and recipes tend that direction. Make sure the plastic bottles don't leak. If you don't use them often, keep them at home and use the oil so it doesn't get old and taste rancid but remember to pack them if you will need them.

Butter keeps quite well at room temperature except that it gets very soft. If you can find it in a small tub, so much the better. If not, place the softened sticks in a small Tupperware container.

Drinks

Proper hydration is always important and never more than when out on the water. I've heard it said that if you haven't urinated in three or four hours, you are on your way to dehydration. I carry my drinking water aboard in the form of bottled water. The water bottles are very sturdy and not prone to chafe and leaking. For cooking and washing fresh water, I carry gallon jugs of fresh water. Another option is a collapsible water jug, found in camping stores. Try and match the amount of water to the time you'll be aboard so the water is used often.

I also carry a variety of other drinks aboard. Most are stored under the starboard quarterberth, next to the hull. This is usually the coolest place aboard, baring the cooler itself. I've gotten used to drinking cool drinks as opposed to ice cold drinks so I don't store a lot of drinks in the cooler.

Under the quarterberth, I have soda, canned juices and spare bottled water. Keep a close eye on how those beverage cans are stored as those pop-tops are vulnerable and can leak if bumped hard enough. If you are in colder climates, remember where you stored all those drinks and remove them from the boat before freezing weather arrives. Otherwise you will have quite a mess to clean up in the spring.

In colder weather, hot chocolate, tea or coffee will be much appreciated. Packets of instant chocolate will be quick to fix and be very welcome on colder sailing days. Use canned or UHT milk instead of water for more depth of flavor and nutrition. Small jars of instant coffee are convenient but I use tea bags for my tea. Coffee junkies may require more elaborate coffee preparation methods but remember the need to properly dispose of the used coffee grounds.

If you carry drinking water in individual bottles, like I do, bring along a selection of individual drink mix packets. I freeze them at the start of a cruise and, after the ice in one has melted, add a drink packet for a cool drink.

Cooking Aboard a Small Boat

Chapter 7: Recipes

Chapter 7: Recipes

Now for the real "meat" of this book, the recipes. In selecting these recipes, I made the assumption that you already have a collection of recipes for the food you eat every day at home, using both fresh ingredients and staples. I would encourage you to use the preceding chapters to adapt those recipes for use aboard your boat. After all, you already know whether you like them or not. These should be used for the fresh and frozen menu items for the first day or two.

Then we go on to the recipes in this chapter, those made from the rest of the kinds of ingredients carried aboard. In the recipes that use meat, you can use canned or fresh, frozen meat almost interchangeably. Unless otherwise noted, they are designed to serve two people. I've also added the usual cooking method after the recipe title so you can select recipes based on your cooking tools.

Appetizers
Buffalo Chicken Dip (frying pan)

Serves: 2

Ingredients
1 (12.5 oz.) can chicken, drained and shredded
1/4 cup Frank's Hot Sauce
1/4 cup blue cheese dressing (or Ranch if you prefer)
1 (4 oz.) pkg. cream cheese softened

8 oz shredded sharp cheddar, Mont. Jack or a combo

Directions
Place dressing and cream cheese in a small frying pan and heat gently. Stir often to mix. Once mix is bubbling, spread cheddar cheese over the top. Spread cream cheese over the bottom of a frying pan. Combine chicken with hot sauce and spread evenly over that. Sprinkle more cheese on top and cover pan. Heat very gently for 20 minutes. Let stand 10 min. before serving.

Serve with tortilla chips or crackers

Chicken Burrito Rollups (Bowl)

Serves: 3

Ingredients
1 cup sour cream
1/3 cup chunky salsa
1/2 cup chopped red onion
1 (4 oz.) can chopped ripe olives
1 tablespoon chopped fresh cilantro
1/4 teaspoon salt
1/8 teaspoon garlic powder
3 (10-inch) flour tortillas
1 (10 oz.) can Chunk Chicken, drained

Directions

Chapter 7: Recipes

At Home
In bowl, combine sour cream, salsa, onion, olives, cilantro, garlic powder and salt; mix well. Spread about 1/2 cup sour cream mixture over each tortilla; top evenly with chicken. Roll tightly; wrap in plastic wrap. Refrigerate several hours or overnight.

At the Boat
Unwrap; slice with a serrated knife to serve.

Quick and Easy Quesadillas (frying pan)

Serves: 2

Ingredients
4 flour Tortillas
Grated cheddar cheese
1 (4 oz.) can sliced olives, drained
1 small onion, chopped
Salsa

Directions
Spray frying pan with a little cooking spray
Fry tortilla until warmed
Flip tortilla
Spread cheddar cheese on top of tortilla
Add chopped onions, sliced olives and salsa on top of cheese (go easy on the salsa or it will get sloppy)
Fold tortilla in half
Continue heating until the tortilla bottom is crispy
Flip tortilla and fry on other side until cheese melts

Slide out of frying pan onto a plate
Cut quesadilla in quarters and serve while hot
Make the next one!

Add-on & Upgrades: Add 1 (5 oz.) can cooked
chicken, shredded.

Quick Pizza Appetizers (frying pan)

Serves: As many as you want to make

Ingredients:
1 jar pasta sauce
1 onion, chopped
1 can sliced olives
1 package peperoni slices
Oregano
Granulated garlic
Shredded mozzarella cheese
Flour tortillas
Cooking oil

Directions
Sauté peperoni slices until they release some of their oil
Sauté chopped onions with the peperoni
Add the pasta sauce and heated through
Season with oregano, salt, pepper and garlic
Spread layer on flour tortillas
Add shredded cheese to tortilla

Fold tortilla in half and place in frying pan with a little oil.

Cook on both sides until tortilla is browned and cheese has melted

Slide onto a serving plate and cut into four pieces

Breakfast
Beefy Scrambled Eggs (frying pan)

Serves: 4

Ingredients
1/2 (4.5 oz.) jar dried beef
6 large eggs, lightly beaten
1 (4 oz.) package cream cheese, cubed
1 tablespoon chopped fresh parsley
1/4 teaspoon pepper
1 tablespoon butter or margarine

Directions
Rinse dried beef with boiling water; drain. Chop into small pieces. In bowl, combine beef, eggs, cream cheese, parsley and pepper; mix well. In frying pan, melt butter over medium heat. Add egg mixture; cook, stirring occasionally, until cheese is melted and eggs are cooked.

Boater's Breakfast Hash (frying pan)

Serves: 2

Ingredients
1/4 cup butter, cubed
1/2 (20 oz.) package - shredded hash browns
1/2 (7 oz.) package - Li'l Smokies sausages
1 small onion, chopped
5 eggs, lightly beaten
Salt and pepper to taste
1 cup shredded cheddar cheese

Directions
At Home
Place hash browns and sausages in a Ziploc bag and freeze.

On the Boat
Melt butter in a large skillet. Add potatoes, sausage and onion. Cook uncovered over medium heat for 10-15 minutes, turning once. Push potato mixture to the sides of the pan. Pour eggs into center of pan. Cook and stir over medium heat until eggs are completely set. Season with salt and pepper. Stir eggs into potato mixture. Top with cheese and cook for 1-2 minutes longer.

Chipped Beef on Toast (pot)

A sure-fire cure for a cold morning aboard.

Serves: 2

Chapter 7: Recipes

Figure 49: Chipped beef on toast makes a hearty breakfast.

Ingredients:

1 (2.5-oz.) package Hormel® Sliced Dried Beef,
chopped or
½ Jar canned dried beef
2 tablespoons butter or margarine
2 tablespoons all-purpose flour
1-1/3 cups milk
1/2 teaspoon Worcestershire sauce
1/2 teaspoon pepper
2 slices toast

Directions

In skillet, cook dried beef in butter 3 minutes. Stir in
flour; add milk. Cook and stir until thickened and

bubbly. Cook and stir 1 to 2 minutes longer. Stir in Worcestershire sauce and pepper. Spoon over toast.

(Recipe adapted from Hormel Foods)

Pancakes in a Sack (frying pan)

Serves: 2

Ingredients
1-1/2 cups all-purpose flour
1 teaspoon white or yellow cornmeal
1 teaspoon brown sugar
1/8 teaspoon salt
3/4 teaspoon baking soda
1 teaspoon baking powder
1 egg
1 cups milk
Nonstick cooking spray

Directions
Mix the dry ingredients at home and place in a Ziploc bag. On the boat, mix all ingredients together in the bag until blended but still lumpy. Preheat and then spray frying pan. Spoon batter into pan. Fry until golden brown then flip and fry other side.

Recipe adapted from "The One Pan Galley Gourmet"

Oatmeal Extraordinaire (pot)

Serves: 2

Ingredients
1-1/2 cups water
1/8 teaspoon salt (optional)
1/3 cup old-fashioned oatmeal or steel-cut oats
1/4 cup raisins
2 tablespoons brown sugar
1/4 cup walnuts

Directions
Over a medium flame, bring the water and salt (if desired) to a boil. Add oats, stirring slowly to prevent lumping. Cook for 5 minutes (15 minutes for steel cut) or until all water is absorbed. Add raisins and cook for another 2 to 3 minutes, stirring occasionally. When ready to eat, stir in brown sugar and walnuts.

Recipe adapted from "The One Pan Galley Gourmet"

Spruced-Up Scrambled Eggs (frying pan)

Serves: 2

Ingredients
5 large eggs

1/4 cup milk (fresh or UHT)
Salt and pepper to taste
Nonstick cooking spray
Extras (see following list)

Directions
Beat eggs, milk, and salt and pepper in a bowl. Spray
frying pan and heat over medium heat. Pour eggs into
pan and let cook undisturbed for about 30 seconds.
Add desired extras and mix in with spatula. Cook for 2
minutes, scraping bottom of pan as you continue to
turn the eggs until dry (or as done as you like).

Adds & Upgrades
Meat
    Diced ham or steak
    Sliced hot dog, bologna, or salami
    Chicken chunks

Cheese
    Diced block cheese
    Cubed cream cheese

Spices
    Tabasco sauce
    Oregano
    Basil

If you're an egg fanatic, there are ways to make the dependable, edible egg more exciting. Try adding dried mushrooms, parsley, onions, or green peppers. For spice, add a few tablespoons of medium or hot salsa. Or put crunch into your meal with walnuts, cashews, or peanuts. And if you're really adventurous, try adding dried fruits, such as apricots, along with nuts.

Adapted from "The One Pan Galley Gourmet"

Sandwiches & Wraps

Figure 50: Chicken Caesar Salad wraps can be made at home, wrapped in aluminum foil and refrigerated for serving aboard your boat.

Chicken Caesar Salad Wraps (bowl)

I sometimes make these ashore, wrap them in aluminum foil and refrigerate them. Great for lunch or dinner on the first or second day aboard.

Serves: 4

Ingredients

1 (10 oz.) can Hormel® Chunk Breast of Chicken, drained and flaked
2 cups thinly sliced romaine lettuce
1 medium tomato, diced
1/4 cup fat-free creamy Caesar salad dressing
1 tablespoon grated Parmesan cheese
4 fajita-size flour tortillas

Directions
In large bowl, combine chicken, lettuce, tomato, dressing and cheese; toss until well combined. Divide chicken mixture evenly among tortillas; wrap tortillas around filling.

Chinese Chicken Salad (bowl)

Serves: 4

Ingredients
2 tablespoons sesame seeds
2 (14.5 oz.) can chicken, chopped (or use rotisserie chicken) or 1 lb. shrimp, cooked, cleaned, chopped
1 small head cabbage, chopped
1 small onion, minced
1/2 cup slivered almonds
1 package chicken or shrimp flavored Top Ramen Noodles, broken up
2 tablespoons sugar
1/4 teaspoon freshly ground black pepper
1/2 teaspoon salt
1/3 cup olive oil

2 tablespoons sesame oil
Flavor packet from noodles

Directions
Combine sesame seeds, chicken or shrimp, onions, almonds, and noodles in a large plastic bowl with tight fitting lid. In a cup, combine sugar, pepper, salt , olive and sesame oils, and seasoning packet from noodles. Whisk to mix and then pour over salad mixture. Mix well, cover, and chill before serving. Keeps for 3-5 days if well-refrigerated.

From the SaltySailor website

Chunky BBQ Sandwiches (pot)

1 (4.5 oz.) can Beef, Pork, Chicken, or Turkey
1/2 (16 oz.) bottle BBQ Sauce
Additional water as needed

DO NOT DRAIN MEAT, Do Not Shred Meat; it will break apart while stirring. Place meat in large saucepan or skillet. Pour BBQ sauce over meat. Add water as needed to thin mixture. Simmer and stir until mixture is hot and consistency you like. The BBQ should be shiny.

Corned Beef Salad (bowl)

Chapter 7: Recipes

Canned Corned Beef with the addition of tomato, onion, mayo and a touch of barbecue sauce makes a great meat salad for sandwiches or crackers

Serves: 2 (1/2 cup each)

Ingredients

1/2 (6 oz.) can Libby's® Corned Beef
1/4 cup chopped fresh tomato
3 tablespoons chopped white onion
3 tablespoons light mayonnaise
1 tablespoon Hunt's® Original Barbecue Sauce
Ground black pepper and salt to taste
Bread or crackers, optional

Directions

Crumble corned beef in medium bowl. Add tomato, onion, mayonnaise, barbecue sauce, black pepper and salt; mix well. Serve on bread or crackers, if desired.

Tasty Chicken Salad (bowl)

Serves: 2

Ingredients
1 (14.5 oz.) can chicken drained and diced
1/4 cup honey
1/4 cup vegetable oil

Juice of 1 lemon
1/2 teaspoon onion salt (optional)
2 stalks celery, diced
1 tablespoon Dijon mustard
1-1/2 cups chop suey noodles

Directions
In a bowl, whisk together all ingredients except chicken and noodles. Add chicken and noodles and toss to coat with dressing. Serve on buns, bread or pita bread.

Adapted from "The One Pan Galley Gourmet"

Sides
Barbecue Beans (pot)

Serves 2

Figure 51: Barbeque Beans served in a heavy-weather serving dish.

Ingredients:

1 (15 oz.) can Pork &Beans
1 (5 oz.) can Vienna Sausages in Barbecue Sauce
1-tablespoon dried onion flakes
2-tablespoons Ketchup
1-teaspoon Mustard
1/4 teaspoon chili powder
Dash Frank's Hot Sauce (optional)

Directions:

Add ingredients to pot
Heat until onion flakes are rehydrated

Hot German Potato Salad (pot)

Serves: 2

Ingredients
1 (14 oz.) can sliced potatoes
3 slices bacon, cut into ½" pieces
1 small onion, chopped
1 tablespoon all-purpose flour
1-1/2 teaspoon white sugar
1 teaspoon salt
1/4 teaspoon celery flakes

Ground black pepper to taste
Water from canned potatoes
1/4 cup distilled white vinegar

Directions

At Home
Chop onion and bacon and place in separate Ziploc bag, then refrigerate

On Boat
Drain canned potatoes, reserve liquid
Sauté bacon in frying pan until crisp
Add onions, cook until translucent
Add flour, cook for 3 to 5 minutes while stirring
Add vinegar, sugar, salt, celery flakes and reserved liquid
Stir while sauce thickens, add water as necessary
Add sliced potatoes and continue to cook until sauce is thick and potatoes are warmed through

---

Instant Garlic Mashed Potatoes (pot)

Servings: 2

Ingredients:
1 cup water
3/4 teaspoon garlic salt
1/2 tablespoon butter or margarine
1/2 cup UHT milk
1 cup instant potato flakes

Directions:
Boil water in a medium saucepan. Meanwhile, mix potato flakes and garlic salt. Add boiling water to potato flakes. Stir in milk and butter or margarine.

Mexican Rice (pot)

Serves: 2 as a main dish, 4 as a side dish

Mexican Rice can be prepared as a side dish or main dish. Cooking rice aboard can be a problem especially if you are a rice snob like me. I prefer Basmati-style rice which requires longer cooking and some simmering. I usually prepare the rice at home and seal it in a bag for use in this recipe. The other option is to use quick cooking Minute Rice. Adding a can of Hormel Chunk Chicken or Ham will turn this side dish into a main course.

Ingredients
2-cups cooked rice
1 (8 oz.) can tomato sauce or tomato paste (use tomato paste if you like a more intense tomato flavor)
1 (4 oz.) can chopped green chilies
Water as needed
2-tablespoons dried onion flakes
1-tablespoon chili powder

1-teaspoon granulated garlic
1-teaspoon ground cumin
¼-teaspoon oregano
2 chicken bouillon cubes
Dash Frank's Hot Sauce (if desired)

Directions

Combine tomato paste or sauce, spices and chopped chilies in a sauce pan. Add water to form a thick sauce (if using tomato sauce, use just enough water to rinse out the can). Simmer until sauce is heated and spices are reconstituted. Stir in rice and heat through.

Adds & Upgrades:

You can add a can or Hormel Chunk Chicken or Ham to turn into a main course. You can also add a 4 oz. can of sliced black olives if desired.

Thermos Bottle Pasta (wide-mouth thermos)

I make this in my Stanley 24 oz. stainless steel wide mouth thermos bottle.

Serves: 2

Ingredients:

Hot water
Handful of spaghetti or other pasta
Salt
Olive oil

Directions:

Fill thermos with boiling water to preheat. Dump the water and place pasta in the thermos. You will probably have to break the pasta in half to get it in the thermos, if you are using spaghetti. Add a dash of salt and a little olive oil to keep the pasta from sticking together. Fill thermos with boiling water and cap. Give the thermos a shake to distribute the salt and olive oil. Let it sit for around two hours. You will need to try this at home a couple of times to get the right level of al dente in your pasta.

Three Bean Salad (bowl)

Serves: 4

Ingredients
1 (15 oz.) can green beans, rinsed and drained
1 (15 oz.) can kidney beans, rinsed and drained
1 (15 oz.) can garbanzo beans, rinsed and drained
1 small onion, chopped fine
2 tablespoons dried parsley
1 bottle Italian or other favorite salad dressing

Directions

Mix canned vegetables, onion and parsley in a bowl. Add salad dressing and season to taste with salt and pepper. Prepare ahead of time and let the salad marinate.

Soups & Stews

Big Time Beef Stew (pot)

Serves:2

Ingredients

1 (14.5 oz.) can beef, liquid reserved

1/2 cup flour

1 to 2 tablespoons vegetable oil

1-1/2 cups water (including reserved liquids)

1 (15 oz.) can whole potatoes, cubed, reserve liquid

I small onion, cut in chunks

1 carrot, cut in chunks

Salt and pepper to taste

I bay leaf

1 teaspoon Worcestershire sauce

Celery flakes to taste

1 package McCormick Onion Gravy mix

1 egg, beaten

Directions

Over medium heat, sauté onion in a tablespoon of oil, turning to prevent sticking. Sprinkle the Onion Gravy mix and add water. Cook while stirring and scraping bottom with spoon. Add all other ingredients except beef, cover, and simmer at least 30 minutes. Stir occasionally. Add beef. Add a little water, a few dashes of vegetable oil, and the beaten egg to flour. Mix into a sticky dough. With oiled spoon, drop balls of dough into stew, cover pan again, and cook 5 more minutes. Do not stir stew after you add the dumplings.

Adapted from "The One Pan Galley Gourmet"

Capt'n Pauley's Tortellini Soup (pot)

Serves: 4

This recipe has evolved over the years to be a quick to prepare soup for those cold days on the water. It is even better is prepared ahead of time and the tortellini added the day of serving (the tortellini gets too soggy is added too soon).

Ingredients
1/2 Lb. Italian sausage, sweet or half sweet and half hot, bulk or removed from casing
1 cup beef broth (water + 1 bouillon ube)
Water as needed
1 (8.5 oz.) can whole kernel corn
1 (15 oz.) cans dark kidney beans
1 (15 oz.) can crushed tomatoes
1 clove garlic, crushed

1 teaspoon fennel seed
1 8 oz. package tortellini of desired flavor
Salt and pepper to taste

Directions

At Home
Brown sausage, cool, place in a Ziploc bag and freeze.

On the Boat
Add sausage to pot. Add canned vegetables (including liquid from cans) and spices. Simmer for about 20 minutes, Add tortellini and simmer until tortellini is done. Add water as needed. Adjust seasoning to taste

---

Chesapeake Clam Chowder (pot)

You could just open a can of Campbell's Clam Chowder but what fun is that? BTW, if you sail on the Chesapeake Bay, you are required to carry Old Bay Seasoning aboard.

Serves: 2

Ingredients

2 (6.5 oz.) can chopped clams
1 (15 oz.) can whole new potatoes
1 (5 oz.) can evaporated milk
3 strips chopped bacon
1 small chopped onion

Old Bay Seasoning
Salt and pepper to taste
1 tablespoon flour

Directions

At Home
Chop bacon and onion and place in separate Ziploc
bags, refrigerate.

On the Boat
Drain the potatoes, reserving the liquid.
Cube potatoes
Fry bacon until crisp
Add onions and cook until translucent
Stir in flour and cook for several minutes
Add reserved potato liquid and evaporated milk
Stir until thickened
Add water if necessary
Add cubed potatoes and clams and heat through
Season with Old Bay Seasoning

Chicken-Chili Stew (pot)

Serves: 2

Figure 52: None of the ingredients for Chicken-Chili Stew require refrigeration.

Ingredients

1 (19.5 oz.) can chicken corn chowder chunky soup
1 (4.5 oz.) can chopped green chilies
1 (5 oz.) can chicken chunks
1-tablespoons dried minced onion
¼-teaspoon garlic powder
1/8-teaspoon oregano
Salt and pepper to taste

Water – if needed to thin mixture out.

Directions

Open cans, add all ingredients to a pan and heat until onion stops crunching.

Chicken Mushroom Casserole (pot)

Serves: 4

Ingredients
1 (14.5 oz.) can chicken, liquid reserved
1 (10 3/4 oz.) can cream of mushroom soup
1 (10 3/4 oz.) can cream of chicken soup
1 (6 oz.) can sliced mushrooms, liquid reserved
1 (8 oz.) carton sour cream
1/4 cup - butter (melted)
1/2 to 1 cup - crushed potato chips

Directions
Heat soups, mushrooms and sour cream in a medium saucepan until boiling; remove from heat and add chicken. Heat 20 minutes, until bubbly. Serve over rice, noodles, mashed potatoes or biscuits.

Chicken Paprika (pot)

Serves: 2

Cooking Aboard a Small Boat

Ingredients
1(14.5 oz.) can chicken
 salt and pepper to taste
 garlic powder to taste
 2 tablespoons peanut oil
1 medium onion, thinly sliced
I medium tomato, chopped
2 chicken bouillon cubes
I cup water
1 tablespoon paprika (Hungarian is best)
112 cup uncooked Minute Rice

Directions
Rub chicken with salt, pepper, and garlic powder. To
preheated pan, add oil and chicken. Brown chicken on
both sides. Add onion and cook for 2 to 3 minutes.
Add tomato, bouillon cubes, and water. Bring to boil.
Add paprika and stir. Cover and cook for 10 minutes
over medium heat. Five minutes before serving, add
Minute Rice to simmering sauce. Cook for I minute
and let stand 4 minutes, covered (make sure all rice is
soaking in sauce, or else you'll find some unexpected
crunch).

Adapted from "The One Pan Galley Gourmet"

Chapter 7: Recipes

Chili Blast (pot)

Serves: 2

Ingredients
1 pound stew beef or steak, cut into'/1-inch cubes
1 small onion, chopped
1 clove garlic, minced
2 tablespoons vegetable oil
1 (15 oz.) can corn, drained
1 (5 oz.) can tomato paste
1-1/4 cups water
2 chili peppers (mild or hot), seeded and chopped
1/4 teaspoon salt (optional)
 Spices to taste (cumin, coriander, or chili powder)

Directions
In frying pan, cook onion, beef, and garlic in oil until
beef is browned. Add all other in ingredients. Bring to
boil and reduce heat. Simmer covered for about 30
minutes or until meat is tender.

Adapted from "The One Pan Galley Gourment"

Creamy Chicken Stew with Vegetables (pot)

Serves: 2

Cooking Aboard a Small Boat

Ingredients
1 (14.5 oz.) can chicken
4 rounded tablespoons nonfat powdered milk
1 (6 oz.) can mushrooms, reserve liquid
1 level tablespoon white flour
1 cups water (including reserved mushroom liquid)
1 cup canned, chopped vegetables of your choice, such as potatoes, onions, green beans, carrots
2 large cloves sliced garlic
1 teaspoons black pepper

Directions
Boil all ingredients except milk powder and flour for 20 minutes or until chicken is heated through. Mix milk powder and flour with a 1/2 cup water and add to pot. Boil two more minutes. Serve in large bowls. Reheat leftovers in the morning.

From Atomvoyages.com

Easy Crab Bisque (pot)

Serves: 4

Ingredients
1 (11.5 oz.) can condensed cream of mushroom soup
1 (11.5 oz.) can condensed cream of celery soup
3/4 cup half and half or milk
1(16 oz.) can lump crab meat
¼ cup dry sherry or Madeira, according to taste
1/8 teaspoon ground white pepper

1 tablespoon butter
¼ teaspoon Old Bay Seasoning

Directions
Combine all ingredients and bring to a boil. Reduce heat and simmer for 5 minutes. Serve in bowls. Sprinkle top of soup with as much Old Bay Seasoning as you like, and have saltines or crackers of your choice with the soup.

Adapted from *"The Frugal Yacht"*

Paul's Goulash (pot)

Serves: 2

Ingredients:

1 (14.5 oz.) can beef
 Salt and pepper to taste
I large onion, diced
1 tablespoon butter or cooking oil
1/2 teaspoon oregano
1/2 teaspoon garlic powder
1/2 teaspoon basil
I teaspoon sugar
1 fresh tomato, cubed (optional)
I (6 oz.) can tomato paste
I cup liquid

2 cups precooked macaroni or rice

Directions:

Cook macaroni or rice in your thermos. Open canned beef and drain broth. Add enough water to make one cup liquid. Sauté onions with butter or oil until onions are soft. Add remaining ingredients except macaroni; stir until tomato paste is dissolved. Simmer for 10 minutes. Season with salt and pepper to taste. Add macaroni or rice and beef and then stir until hot. Beef is very tender so don't over-stir. Serve with Parmesan cheese and French bread.

Pronto Chili (pot)

Serves: 4

Ingredients
1 (14.5 oz.) can beef
1 small onion, chopped
3-4 teaspoon chili powder
1 teaspoon ground cumin
¼ teaspoon oregano
1 teaspoon salt
1 (14.5 oz.) can Mexican stewed tomatoes
1 (15 oz.) can chili beans
1 (15 oz.) can whole kernel corn
Shredded cheddar cheese, optional

Directions
In a pot, cook, onion until tender. Add the next 7 ingredients, cover and simmer for 20 min. Add meat to the pot and simmer until heated. Do not over-stir as beef is very tender. Sprinkle individual servings with cheese if desired.

Quickie Chili (pot)

McCormick makes five different chili seasoning mixes. This one is the hottest. If you don't like your chili spicy, choose one of the other blends.

Serves: 4

Ingredients
Frozen precooked ground beef (1 lb. uncooked)
1 (15 oz.) can kidney beans
1 (14.5 oz.) can crushed tomatoes
I package McCormick Hot Chili seasoning mix.

Directions
Place all ingredients in a pot. Bring to a boil. Reduce heat and simmer for 10 minutes.

Adds & Upgrades

Add I small onion, chopped or 1 (4 oz.) chopped green chillies.

Ternabout's White Chili (pot)

Serves: 2

Ingredients

1 (15.5 oz.) can great northern beans
1 (4 oz.) can chopped green chilies
1/4-teaspoon garlic powder
1/8-teaspoon black pepper
2 tablespoon dried minced onions
2 teaspoon dried celery flakes
1/8-teaspoon oregano
2 (5 oz.) cans chicken

Directions

Dump all ingredients except chicken into a saucepan, preferably non-stick. Bring mixture to a boil and reduce to a simmer. Simmer for 30 to 40 minutes, until dried onion is reconstituted and mixture is thoroughly heated. Add chicken; continue cooking until chicken is heated. Do not overcook. If you have it, add a half of cup of shredded Monterey Jack cheese just before serving.

Ternabout's Gumbo (pot)

Serves: 2

Ingredients

1-tablespoon cooking oil
1-tablespoon flour
1 (14.5 oz.) can diced tomatoes
1 can water
1/4 cup uncooked rice
1/8-teaspoon black pepper
1/4-teaspoon garlic powder
1 bay leaf
1-teaspoon parsley flakes
2 tablespoon dried diced onions
1 teaspoon dried celery flakes
1-teaspoon chicken bouillon
1/2 teaspoon Cajun seasoning, Tabasco, cayenne
pepper or other seasoning to desired heat
1 (5 oz.) canned ham, cut into bite-sized pieces
1 (5 oz.) canned chicken

Directions

Place oil and flour in a non-stick saucepan and cook to
a golden brown. Add diced tomatoes and one half the
water. Add spices, seasoning and rice. Simmer for 30
to 40 minutes or until rice is tender. Add water as
necessary, make it as thick or thin as you like. Just
before serving, add canned meat and allow warming
through.

Main Courses
Basic Spaghetti Sauce (pot)

Serves: 2

This is a basic sauce that can be fixed quickly from stores, staples and spices you have on hand. Serve it over pasta, rice or noodles. You can also add any of the add-ons for a more filling meal or for more servings.

Ingredients
1 (8 oz.) can tomato sauce
Water to rinse can
1 tablespoon dried onion flakes
½ tablespoon parsley flakes
½ teaspoon dried oregano
½ teaspoon granulated garlic
Salt and pepper to taste
Dash or two of Frank's Hot Sauce if desired

Directions

Add all items to a sauce pan. Rinse out the can with a small amount of water and add to the pan. Simmer long enough to reconstitute the dried spices. Pour over pasta and serve.

Adds & Upgrades

1-small can mushrooms

Handful of hamburger–flavored TVP

1-can drained tuna fish

Beef Stroganoff (pot)

Serves: 2

Ingredients

1 (14.5 oz.) can beef

1 (6 oz.) can mushrooms, drained

1 medium chopped onion

2 tablespoons flour

1 teaspoon instant beef bouillon

1/2 teaspoon salt

1/2 teaspoon prepared mustard

Dash of pepper

1/2 cup buttermilk or plain yogurt

2 teaspoons parsley flakes

Directions

Crumble beef into a pot. Add mushrooms and onions. Cook, uncovered, for 7 to 8 minutes, stirring twice. Stir in flour, bouillon, salt, mustard, pepper and 1 cup of water. Cook, covered, for 7 minutes, stirring once. Stir in buttermilk and parsley. Cook, covered, for 2 to 3 minutes or until hot.

Can be served over noodles.

Bully Beef (frying pan)

Serves: 4

Ingredients
1 (12 oz.) can Corned Beef (Bully Beef)
1 clove garlic
½ teaspoon black pepper
1 medium onion, chopped
1 hot pepper (Scotch Bonnet, if you dare)
1 Tomato, chopped
1/8 teaspoon dried thyme
3 tablespoons water

Directions
Combine the beef, garlic and black pepper in a bow; and mix together well. Heat some oil in a frying pan. Add the onion, hot pepper, tomato and thyme. Fry gently for about 10 minutes, stirring occasionally. Add the beef mixture and the water to the pan. Fry gently for another 5 minutes, stirring occasionally.

Chapter 7: Recipes

Chicken a la King (pot)

Serves: 2

Ingredients

1 (6 oz.) can mushrooms (reserve 1/4 cup liquid)
1/4 cup butter or margarine
1/4 cup flour
1/2 teaspoon salt
¼ teaspoon pepper
1 (5 oz.) can evaporated milk
1 cup chicken broth (reserved liquid from canned
chicken and mushrooms)
1 14.5 oz. can chicken, cubed, reserve liquid
1 (4 oz.) jar Pimento, chopped

Directions

Cook and stir mushrooms in butter 5 minutes. Blend in
flour, salt & pepper. Cook over low heat, stirring until
mixture is bubbly. Remove from heat; stir in cream,
broth and reserved mushroom liquid. Heat to boiling,
stirring constantly. Boil and stir 1 minute. Stir in
chicken and pimento; heat through. Serve hot over
toast or biscuits, 4 small servings or 2 large servings.

Calcutta Chicken (frying pan)

Serves: 2

Ingredients
1(14.5 oz.) can chicken, cubed
4 tablespoons butter or margarine
1 medium onion, finely chopped
I stalk celery, finely chopped
1/3 cup flour
2 chicken bouillon cubes dissolved in 1-1/2 cups water
1 (6 oz.) can tomato juice
1/2 teaspoon Worcestershire sauce
I teaspoon curry powder
Precooked rice

Directions
Over medium flame, melt the butter and sauté
vegetables until tender. Add chicken and cook
thoroughly, stirring occasionally. Add flour and stir to
mix. Add bouillon mixture immediately, and cook
until sauce is smooth and thick. Add tomato juice,
curry powder, and Worcestershire. Cover and simmer
for 5 minutes. Serve over precooked rice. (Cook, rinse,
stir in a little oil to keep it from clumping, and chill in
a plastic bag.)

Recipe adapted from "The One Pan Galley Gourmet".

Chicken Enchiladas with Green Chile Sauce (frying pan)

Serves: 4

Ingredients
1 (10 oz.) can chunk chicken
1 (4 oz.) can Diced Green Chilies
1/2 cup diced onions
1 cup shredded Mexican blend cheese, divided
1 (10 oz.) can Green Enchilada Sauce
1/4 cup sour cream
4 6 inch flour tortillas

Directions
Combine chicken, green chilies, onion and 1/2 cup shredded cheese in a bowl. In another bowl, combine enchilada sauce and sour cream until well blended. Add 1/2 cup enchilada sauce mixture to chicken mixture. Spread a small amount of enchilada sauce mixture over bottom of frying pan. Evenly divide chicken mixture down the center of each tortilla. Roll tortillas up and place seam-side-down in frying pan. Pour remaining enchilada sauce mixture over tortillas. Sprinkle with remaining 1½ cups cheese. Heat gently 25 to 30 minutes or until heated through.

Chicken N Rice (pot)

Serves: 2

Ingredients
2 cups cooked rice
1 (11 oz.) can mushroom soup

2 cups - chicken broth or milk
1 pkg - onion seasoning mix
1/4 cup - butter
1 (14.5 oz.) can chicken

Directions
Sauté mushrooms in butter. Add rice, soup, broth or milk and onion seasoning mix into pot. Heat until bubbling. Add chicken and heat through.

Chicken Pasta Salad (bowl)

Serves: 2

This is a great lunch-time meal for the first or second day out. Prepare the chicken and pasta at home and then mix on the beach after you pull up for lunch.

Ingredients
2 medium boneless chicken breasts
2 cups precooked pasta or macaroni
1 small bag salad greens
1 tomato, chopped
3 green onions chopped
Italian salad dressing
Oregano
Salt and Pepper
Old Bay Seasoning
2 tablespoons olive oil

Directions

At Home
Precook pasta. Cube chicken and fry in olive oil.
Season heavily with Old Bay Seasoning. Place chicken
and pasta in separate Ziplocs and chill.

At the Boat
Combine all ingredients in a bowl and toss to coat
with salad dressing. Season with oregano, salt and
pepper.

Chicken Tetrazzini (pot)

Servings: 4

Ingredients

1/4 cup - butter
1/2 teaspoon- salt
Chicken broth (Drained from canned chicken)
1 can - pasteurized process cheese
1 (14.5 oz.) can chicken
1 can - mushroom soup
1/4 cup - flour
1/4 teaspoon- pepper
1 cup - half and half, evaporated milk or UHT milk
1/2 lb - angel hair spaghetti, cooked and drained

Directions

Cook spaghetti ahead of time in a wide-mouth thermos. Melt butter in large saucepan over low heat. Blend in flour, salt and pepper. Cook over low heat stirring until smooth and bubbly and slightly browned. Remove from heat. Stir in broth, cream, soup and cheese, heat to boiling. Boil and stir for 1 minute. Stir in spaghetti and chicken and heat until warmed through.

Adds & Upgrades:
Add 1-6 oz. can sliced mushrooms

Creamed Chicken and Noodles (pot)

Serves: 2

Ingredients
2 chicken bouillon cubes
1-1/2 cups water
2 boneless chicken breasts (or softpack), cut in chunks
4 ounces cream cheese
1 (15 oz.) can peas, drained
2 tablespoons flour
1 cup precooked noodles or macaroni

Directions
Precook noodles or macaroni in pot or thermos. In pot, bring bouillon cubes and water to boil. Add all other ingredients (add cream cheese a chunk at a time).

Reduce heat, cover, and simmer for 30 minutes. Stir occasionally. Serve over precooked noodles.

Adapted from "The One Pan galley Gourmet"

Curried Beef (pot)

Serves: 2

Ingredients
1 tablespoon olive oil
1-3/4 pound sirloin cut in 1-inch cubes
1 medium onion, chopped
1/2 tablespoon curry powder
1/2 teaspoon salt (optional)
1/3 cup unsalted peanuts
1 beef bouillon cube

Directions
In a frying pan, add oil and brown meat and vegetables over medium heat. Drain oil. Add curry powder and mix well. Mix in salt (if desired) and nuts. Add 1/3 cup water and bouillon cube to meat mixture and simmer for 15 minutes. Serbe over rice.

Adapted from "The One Pan Galley Gourmet"

Easy Chicken & Cheese Enchiladas (frying pan)

Serves: 6

I usually fix the enchiladas at home and place them in a Ziploc. I can then finish heating them aboard the boat. The good thing is you don't have to fix them all at once, you can feed anywhere from 2 to 6 people of multiple meals.

Ingredients
1 (11-1/2 oz.) can Cream of Chicken soup
½ cup sour cream
1 cup Pace Picante Sauce
2 teaspoons chili powder
2 cups chopped chicken
½ cup shredded Monterey Jack cheese
6 flour tortillas
1 small tomato, chopped
1 green onion, sliced

Directions

At Home
Stir the soup, sour cream, picante sauce and chili powder in a medium bowl. Stir 1 cup of picante sauce mixture, chicken and cheese in a large bowl. Divide chicken mixture among tortillas. Roll up the tortillas and place them in a Ziploc bag. Pour the remaining picante sauce in another Ziploc bag, Refrigerate or freeze both.

On the Boat
Place the desired number of tortillas in your frying
pan. Pour picante sauce mixture over tortillas. Cover
the frying pan with aluminum foil if you don't have a
lid. Heat tortillas until enchiladas are hot and
bubbling. Top with tomato and onion.

Linguini with Clam Sauce (pot)

Serves: 2

Ingredients
1/4 (16 ounce) package linguine pasta
2 tablespoons butter
1 tablespoon olive oil
3/4 teaspoon minced garlic, or to taste
1 small onion, chopped
1 (6.5 ounce) can minced clams, drained with juice
reserved
3/4 teaspoon cornstarch, or as needed
1/4 cup chicken broth (water +1 bouillon cube)
1/2 teaspoon cayenne pepper, or to taste
Salt to taste
1 tablespoon dried parsley flakes
1 tablespoon grated Parmesan cheese

Directions
Cook pasta in a thermos bottle (see Thermos Bottle
Pasta recipe). Melt the butter with olive oil in a large
skillet over medium heat. Cook and stir the garlic,

onions and minced clams for 5 minutes. Add the reserved clam juice and cook for a few more minutes. In a separate bowl, whisk the cornstarch with part of the chicken broth. Stir the cornstarch mixture into the skillet. Adjust the thickness of the sauce, if needed, by whisking a little more cornstarch with more chicken broth, and adding to the sauce. Stir in the cayenne pepper and salt. Cook over medium heat, stirring occasionally, about 5 minutes. Stir in the parsley; remove from heat. Pour the clam sauce over the drained linguine. Mix well; serve with Parmesan cheese.

Pressure Cooker Curried Rice (pressure cooker)

I found this pressure cooker recipe on the internet. I don't use a pressure cooker aboard Ternabout, so this recipe hasn't been tried by me. Experiment at your own risk!

This will feed a family of 5 Cook in 8 Quart pressure cooker.

Ingredients:
3 cups brown rice
1 large onion
4 carrots
6 small red potatoes
1.5 pounds chicken or meat substitute (I use a vegetarian product called Tenderbits from Loma Linda foods. 1 can)

4 tablespoons butter or oil
5 cups water
4 tablespoons Curry powder. Make your own... It is better than what comes in a can
  1 teaspoon each: Turmeric, Coriander, Red Pepper (Cayenne) Black pepper, Mustard Powder. I like it HOT and put in 6++ tablespoons
2 tablespoons. salt

Directions
Brown onion in oil. When translucent, add meat. Cook meat for 5 minutes.
Quarter carrots and halve potatoes. Add to pot. Add curry and stir until all is coated. Add rice and stir until coated. Add water and put on lid. Cook over high until pressurized and then turn down. Cook 30 minutes.

Serve with Raita

1 Pint yogurt
1 lemon
½ red onion sliced thin
1 cucumber peeled and sliced thin.
Salt

Quickie Beef Stroganoff (pot)

Serves: 2

Ingredients

1 (12 oz.) can Hormel Roast Beef & Gravy
¼ cup sour cream or 4 oz. Philadelphia Cream Cheese
1 (6 oz.) can sliced mushrooms
¼ teaspoon granulated garlic or garlic powder
Salt and pepper to taste

Directions

Drain gravy from roast beef into a saucepan, reserving meat. Add drained mushrooms, sour cream and garlic. Heat until bubbling. Gently add meat (it is very tender and will break apart if stirred vigorously). Heat until meat is warmed through. Serve over noodles or rice (cooked in thermos or mashed potatoes.

Steak au Poivre (frying pan)

Serves: 2

Ingredients
2 tenderloin steaks, 4 to 6 ounces each and no more than 1/2 to 3/4 inches thick
_Salt
1 tablespoon coarse ground black pepper
1 tablespoon unsalted butter
1 teaspoon olive oil
1/3 cup Cognac, plus 1 teaspoon or same amount of red or white wine
1(5 oz.) can evaporated milk

Directions

Remove the steaks from the refrigerator for at least 30 minutes and up to 1 hour prior to cooking. Sprinkle all sides with salt._Spread the pepper evenly onto a plate. Press the fillets, on both sides, into the pepper until it coats the surface. Set aside.

In your frying pan over medium heat, melt the butter and olive oil. As soon as the butter and oil begin to turn golden and smoke, gently place the steaks in the pan. For medium-rare, cook for 2 minutes on each side. Once done, remove the steaks to a plate, tent with foil and set aside. Pour off the excess fat but do not wipe or scrape the pan clean.

Off of the heat, add 1/3 cup Cognac to the pan and carefully ignite the alcohol with a long match or lighter. Gently shake pan until the flames die. Return the pan to medium heat and add the evaporated milk. Bring the mixture to a boil and whisk until the sauce coats the back of a spoon, approximately 5 to 6 minutes. Add the teaspoon of Cognac and season, to taste, with salt. Add the steaks back to the pan, spoon the sauce over, and serve.

Tuna Macaroni (pot)

Serves: 2

Ingredients
2 cups macaroni

1 (11 oz.) can Campbell's Cream of Mushroom or
Cream of Chicken soup
1(5 oz.) can tuna
½ to 1 cup water or UHT milk
Salt and pepper, to taste

Directions
Precook macaroni in a large pot at home or in your
thermos bottle.. Drain well and then add remaining
ingredients to the pot. Stir to combine, then heat on
medium flame until hot and until flavors are
combined. Season to taste with salt and pepper.

Desserts
Mandarin Cream Cheese Pie (bowl)

Serves: 4

Ingredients

1 (8 oz.) package cream cheese, softened
1 (14 oz.) can Eagle Brand® Sweetened Condensed
Milk
1/3 cup lemon or lime juice
1 teaspoon vanilla extract
1-1/2 cups Kashi Go Lean cereal, crushed
1 (11 oz.) can mandarin orange segments, well drained

Directions

At Home:

Beat cream cheese until fluffy in large bowl. Gradually beat in sweetened condensed milk until smooth. Stir in 1/3 cup lemon juice and vanilla. Store in a Tupperware container and chill.

Place cereal in a Ziploc bag and crush with a rolling pin or the bottom of a heavy skillet.

At the boat
Divide crushed cereal between four small bowls or coffee cups. Compact the cereal at the bottom of the dishes. Divide up the filling between the four dishes. Top the filling with the drained mandarin orange segments.

Mountain House Raspberry Crumble (Pouch)

This is a freeze dried dessert from Mountain House, one of the larger suppliers of backpacker meals. Preparation is simple, boil the amount of water called for in the instructions, open up the pouch, pour the water in and wait for it to rehydrate. Tastes great. The only downside is that the pouch serves 4 people so either invite additional friends or be very hungry!

Palacinka – Czechoslovak Crepes (frying pan)

My paternal grandmother was of Czech/German ancestry but it was my English mother who I remember making these. She made them for Shrove

Tuesday, Pancake Day in England. She sprinkled them with brown sugar and chopped walnuts with a squeeze of lemon juice before rolling up.

Make these at home, roll up and place in a Ziploc bag. You can heat them in a frying pan on the boat, if you like them warm.

Serves: As many as you want to make

Ingredients
2 eggs
1 cup milk
1 table spoon butter, melted
½ teaspoon salt
1 teaspoon sugar
1 cup of flour, sifted
Fruit Preserves, Jam, or Syrup or
Brown sugar, lemon juice and chopped walnuts

Directions
Beat together eggs and milk and butter. Gradually add remaining ingredients of Salt, Sugar, and Flour. If batter still appears a little thick, try adding a little more milk to thin out. Pour ladle full of batter onto lightly greased skillet. Flip or turn over crepe as the batter starts to lightly brown. Place crepe on warm plate and cover with foil or another plate until all six are fried. Place fruit mixture (jelly, preserves, or fruit syrup) or brown sugar mixture onto crepe and roll into tube. If you like, top with whipped cream and serve.

Drinks

Dreamy Creamy Hot Chocolate (pot)

Recipe courtesy Paula Deen

Ingredients
1 (14-ounce) can sweetened condensed milk
1/2 cup unsweetened cocoa
1 1/2 teaspoons vanilla extract
1/8 teaspoon salt
6 1/2 cups hot water
Mini Marshmallows (optional)

Directions
In a large saucepan, combine sweetened condensed milk, cocoa, vanilla and salt; mix well. Over medium heat, slowly stir in water; heat through, stirring occasionally. DO NOT BOIL. Top with marshmallows, if desired.

Tip: Chocolate can be stored in the refrigerator up to 5 days. Mix well and reheat before serving.

High Tide (glass)

Ingredients:
4 oz. orange juice
3 oz. cranberry juice
3 oz. lemon lime soda

Directions
Fill a highball type glass with ice (if available); add orange juice, cranberry juice and lemon lime soda.

(This drink can be enjoyed non-alcoholic or tilted toward the tide by adding a shot of vodka.)

Written by s/v Kaleo, via GalleySwap

Hot Apple Cider Boat Drink (bowl)

From Julie Bostian, former About.com Guide

On those cold days on the water it is always refreshing to have a hot beverage greet you when you come out of the weather. This recipe for hot apple cider is a great boat drink to keep you warm.

Ingredients:
1 quart apple cider
1-1/2 cups cranberry juice
1/2 cup water
1 stick cinnamon
1/2 teaspoon whole allspice
1/2 teaspoon whole cloves

Directions
Combine all ingredients in a two quart casserole dish and cover. Microwave on high for 5-8 minutes or until hot. Strain. Pour into a thermos or other insulated beverage holder. Take out on the boat on a cold day of

waterskiing or wakeboarding. Drink when you need to warm your insides after a cold run in the water.

Hot Ginger Cocoa (pot)

Serves: 1 (one large mug)

Ingredients
1 rounded tablespoon pure cocoa powder
2 thin slices fresh ginger root (or substitute a piece of split dried vanilla pod if you're lucky enough to find some locally grown)
5 rounded tablespoons nonfat powdered milk
2 rounded tablespoons brown sugar (or Aspartame if you're sugar sensitive)
1 mug of water

Directions
Boil the ginger and cocoa powder in the water for about two minutes. Mix the dry ingredients with a couple spoons water and then slowly pour in the boiled cocoa and ginger slices while stirring to prevent dry milk lumps. If you're using a smaller cup, adjust ingredients accordingly.

From Atomvoyages.com

Night-Passage Swiss Mocha Mix (mug)

I found this recipe on the www.saltysailors.com website. I don't drink coffee, so I haven't tried this recipe. You are on your own!

Ingredients
1 cup instant coffee
1 cup sugar
2 cups non-fat dry milk powder
4 teaspoons cocoa

Directions
Mix all ingredients together and store in an airtight container.
Use 2 teaspoons in a cup of hot water.

Chapter 8: Hints, Tips and Tricks

"Baggie Omelets"

I've seen several recipes for "baggie omelets". These are eggs and other ingredients place in a baggie and boiled to cook. It sounds like a great, no-mess way to make an omelet. However, in checking with the makers of the various brands of baggies, they all state that their products are not recommended for "boil in the bag" use. The vacuum sealer bags, like "Seal a Meal" bags are rated for "boil in the bag" use but you won't have the sealer aboard to seal them.

Home Made Gel packs

On several occasions a 'gel' ice pack was needed while cruising. The following is a recipe to make your own gel ice pack:

Contents:
- 2 large Ziploc bags (sliding locks bags tend to leak. Try not to use them)
- Rubbing Alcohol
- Water
- Duct Tape

Ratio: 1 part Rubbing Alcohol 2 parts water

Directions:
Fill Ziplocs with alcohol and water. Bleed out all the air and seal the Ziploc. Put full bag into the 2nd bag. Seal with duct tape and place in freezer.

*** More water will make it firmer, more alcohol will make it slushier.

S/V Evenstar

Enhanced Ramen Noodles
Add a small can of ham, chicken or tuna to you Ramen noodles for a more exciting dish.

Coffee/Tea Creamer
If you like cream and sugar with you coffee or tea, consider keeping a small can of condensed milk at the ready. The sweetened, thickened milk will be just about the right strength when diluted in the hot drink.

Save Water
If you use boil-in-the bags to cook your food, save the hot water for washing up after the meal.

Protect Those Cans and Bottles
I try not to carry many glass jars aboard for fear of breakage. Cans with ring pulls are also easy to damage and cause leaks and food spoilage. Store them in insulated can coolers (coozies) or socks. Socks are cheap at the local dollar store and either of these items cut down on the noise from the cans and bottles moving around.

Save the Instructions
If you repackage things like pancake mix or potato flakes, cut the instruction off the box and place in the

Ziploc with the food. It saves trying to guess what the proportions are.

Some Substitutions
Don't let the lack of an ingredient hold you up. These substitutions were adapted from the book Kitchen Afloat.

1 cup light cream = 1 cup evaporated milk
1 cup milk = ½ cup evaporated milk + ½ cup water
1 tablespoon flour = 1/2 teaspoon cornstarch
1 small onion =_3/4 teaspoon onion powder
1 small garlic clove = ¼ teaspoon garlic powder
1 pound fresh mushrooms = 1 (6 oz.) canned
1-1/2 tablespoons Balsamic vinegar = ¼ cup wine vinegar
1 cup uncooked macaroni = 2 ro 2-1/2 cups cooked

Spice Alternatives
Basil = oregano
Celery seeds = minced celery
Oregano = majoram
Sage = thyme
Chili pepper = cayenne

Sanitizing a Cutting Board
Use a mild bleach or vinegar solution. 1 teaspoon of chlorine bleach to 1 quart of water or 1 tablespoon of vinegar to 5 tablespoons of water.

Cooking Aboard a Small Boat

Filling Ziploc Bags

Filling Ziploc bags with prepared ingredients or sauces at home can be messy. I place the empty bag in an appropriately sized bowl with the top edges of the bag folded over the edge of the bowl. That leaves the center of the bag open for filling. It also keeps any food off of the sealing edges of the bag. Less mess and less fuss.

Alcohol Stove Tip

Anyone who has a canister type non pressurized alcohol boat stove like the Origo knows that alcohol is getting costly these days. I don't know how many times I've left my stove open to cool it off before I could put that round rubber gasket on the canister, then forgot about it completely. A lot of alcohol probably evaporated before I was able to cover it. I made a notched stick that holds my stove open while it cools and what I do now is after shutting off the flame, I take a damp rag and cool off the canister while flipping the rag over till it's cool to the touch. When the canister is cool, I insert the gasket and place a stainless steel weight on it. This stops any evaporation immediately and the stick allows the upper part of the stove to cool down. From: Joe Alves Jr., s/v Trinkka

Crepe Substitutes

You can substitute flour tortillas for crepes in many recipes. The texture and flavor are slightly different, but a small boat isn't an ideal crepe-making environment.

Precooking Hamburger

1. Top Left: sauté hamburger, season with salt, pepper and garlic.
2. Top right: drain excess grease off of cooked hamburger in a colander.
3. Bottom left: pack cooked hamburger into a Ziploc bag. Note how the bag is draped over a bowl to keep sealing surfaces clean and keep the bag from falling over as you fill it.
4. Bottom right: hamburger sealed in Ziploc bag with excess air squeezed out. When cool, freeze.

Grilled Foods

Cooking Aboard a Small Boat

I like to grill up some burgers and brats ahead of time, vacuum seal and freeze them. "At sea" I drop the frozen, sealed items in a pot of boiling water for 4 minutes and I have what tastes like fresh off the grill food.

If the "seas" are rough, I boil water in the tea kettle and place the sealed items in a container. Pour in the water, close the container, and wait about six to seven minutes. Same results!

The food tastes fresh and I'm not cleaning splatter off the cabin walls or cockpit.

Carl Aubele
Compac 19/II
s/v Miss Adventures

Resources

Resources

Recipes by Cooking Method

Bowl

Frying Pan

Pot

Pressure Cooker

Resources

Thermos bottle

Misc

Books

The Care and Feeding of the Sailing Crew - Paperback by Lin Pardey and Larry Pardey

The One-Pan Galley Gourmet: Simple Cooking on Boats by Donald Jacobson

Galley Guru: Effortless Gourmet Cooking Afloat by Lisa Hayden-Miller

Cruising Cuisine: Fresh Food from the Galley by Kay Pastorius

Kitchen Afloat: Galley Management and Meal Preparation by Joy Smith

The Galley: How Things Work by Donald Launer

One Pot Galley Gourmet by Becky Coffield

The Two Burner Gourmet: The Cookbook for Cooking Far from Home by Terry L. Searfoss

The Best Tips From Women Aboard: Edited by Maria Russell

Websites

Bayou Classic (Portable charcoal grills)
     www.thebayou.com/

Brinkman Farms (canned meats)
     brinkmanfarms.com/

CampMor
     www.campmor.com

Defender
     www.defender.com

Forespar
     www.forespar.com/

Galley guru ™ effortless gourmet cooking afloat
     http://www.galleyguru.com/

Hamilton Marine
     www.hamiltonmarine.com

How To Cook On A Boat
     howtocookonaboat.com/

Kelly Kettles
www.kellykettleusa.com/

Magma Products (gas grills)
     www.magmaproducts.com

Resources

Mountain House Foods (backpacking and camping dehydrated foods)
www.mountainhouse.com

REI
www.rei.com

Small Craft Advisor Magazine
www.smallcraftadvisor.com

The Boat Galley
theboatgalley.com/

Walnut Creek Foods (canned meats)
www.walnutcreekfoods.com/eek Foods

Werling & Sons, Inc. (canned meats)
www.werlingandsons.com/

West Marine
www.westmarine.com

Personal Recipes and Notes

Resources

Cooking Aboard a Small Boat

Resources

Cooking Aboard a Small Boat

Resources

22942082R00112

Made in the USA
Lexington, KY
20 May 2013